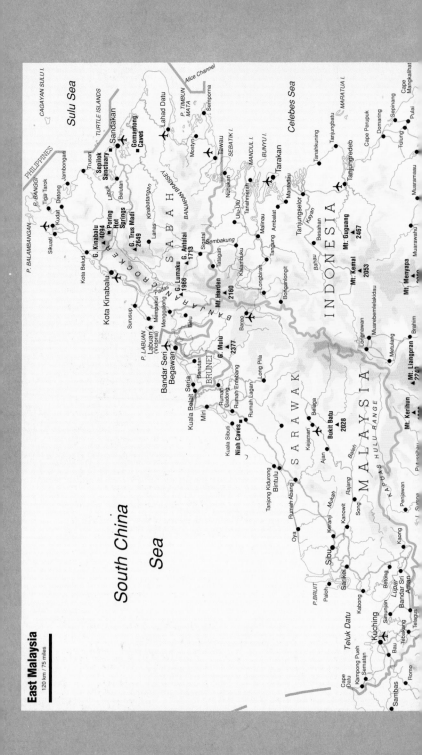

Selamat Datang!

Imagine you have a friend in Sabah, the "Land Below the Wind". She has travelled extensively through the northern tip of Borneo, climbing its mountains, rafting its rivers, discovering the world's most diverse ecosystem in its rainforests, diving pristine coral reefs and staying in remote villages to experience the lifestyle of its many tribal groups. She is delighted to share her love of Sabah with you, guiding you through this richly varied yet little known land.

Your guide, Wendy Hutton, first came to Malaysia in 1967, and has worked in Southeast Asia as a writer and editor ever since. She was involved with Apa Publications in its infancy, contributing to the Insight Guides to Malaysia, Singapore and Java in the early 1970s. She gave in to wanderlust in 1986 when she exchanged her life on land for cruising in Southeast Asian waters where she lives with her partner aboard their trimaran, "Double Dragon".

Hutton introduces you to the history and culture of Sabah, which had ancient trading links with China, was run by a British trading company and become part of the Malaysian Federation in 1963. She suggests 3 half-day itineraries in and around the capital, Kota Kinabalu, then describes 4 day-trips which take you from Southeast Asia's tallest mountain to swamp forest frequented by the unique proboscis monkey, from a wild river to a peaceful beach. These are followed by 4 overnight itineraries, introducing you to the astonishing plant life of the interior, loveable orang-utans, striking hornbills and other remarkable wildlife of the east coast. For the visitor who wants to savour Sabah to the full, there are a further 4 itineraries which demand 3-5 days, owing to both their remote location and remarkable interest.

Suggestions for shopping and practical information are included in the last section of this guide, together with a comprehensive look at the food and restaurants which can provide yet another pleasure during your stay.

Hutton hopes that the suggested itineraries will help the visitor obtain the maximum from a short stay in Sabah, and that this visit will leave him or her with the desire to come back for more.

Selamat Datang! Welcome!

1

Insight Pocket Guide:

Sabah

First Edition

© **1992 APA Publications (HK) Ltd.**

All Rights Reserved

Printed in Singapore by

Höfer Press (Pte) Ltd

Fax: 65-861 6438

SaBaH
Borneo

Written by **Wendy Hutton**

Directed by **Hans Höfer**

Design Concept by **V. Barl**

Art Direction by **Karen Hoisington**

Photography by **Tommy Chang, Wendy Hutton and others**

INSIGHT *Pocket* GUIDES

Contents

Maps

Dear Reader!

When I first came to Sabah almost 15 years ago, I was drawn, like the few other visitors in those days, solely by the magnet of Mount Kinabalu. Inspired by the challenge of climbing the highest peak in Southeast Asia, I raced straight up to Mount Kinabalu, returning to Kota Kinabalu to pause just long enough to swim at Tanjung Aru Beach and gaze back in wonder at the 4,101-metre mountain I had scaled.

It was not until my second, much longer visit that I started to realise how much I had missed in this magnificent corner of Borneo, with its unique wildlife, beautiful rainforests, many rare plants and incredibly welcoming people. When I sailed in yet again a couple of years ago, I intended staying for just three weeks. I seem to have fallen under a spell and have been here ever since, exploring Sabah with ever-increasing delight.

Visitors to Sabah are often astonished that its charms are virtually unknown to the outside world. One pleasant corollary of this is that tourism is a very new concept and visitors are welcomed with genuine hospitality as guests, not as dollar-dispensing tourists.

Nature reigns supreme in Sabah. Don't come here expecting weathered stone temples, classical court dances and other manifestations of an ancient, centralised culture. The challenging terrain dictated that man live in harmony with his environment, in small groups along the coast or in fertile valleys tucked away amongst deeply forested mountain ranges. Although many changes have taken place to both the land and its people this century, Sabah is still very much Borneo, a land of discovery and excitement, where travel can sometimes be challenging but is always rewarding.

Sabah is the Borneo of one's imagination, with massive swamp forests penetrable only by boat, and humid rainforests filled with strange birds and beasts. But this is only the beginning: you'll also find magnificent mountains, exquisite coral-rimmed islands, deserted beaches, lush valleys with babbling brooks. The ardent naturalist will find Sabah a rare paradise; so, too, the amateur anthropologist, who'll be intrigued by the differing lifestyles of Sabah's many ethnic groups. The outdoor enthusiast who enjoys climbing, trekking, scuba diving, swimming, white-water rafting, fishing or golf will never run out of options, while the sybarite in search of a relaxing holiday can laze about exquisite tropical islands with nothing more taxing to do than decide where to dine that evening.

Sabah is only just being discovered by tourism, yet facilities are adequate, if not luxurious, in most areas outside the major centres. There's nothing limited, however, about the hospitality of the Sabahans, who have to be among the world's kindest, most relaxed and hospitable people.

Remember that this is a guide and not a bible, to be used as a starting point and an inspiration for planning a visit to suit your own particular interests. Some of the suggested itineraries overlap, while others can be combined – such as a trip to the Turtle Islands off Sandakan and viewing other wildlife in the Sandakan region.

These itineraries introduce you to just a few of my favourite destinations, lively local markets, non-touristy eating places and romantic hideaways. I hope they will open your eyes to the many possibilities in Sabah, and that you will leave sharing my enthusiasm for this endlessly varied and lovely "Land Below the Wind".

9

Borneo has long nourished the world's dreams and fantasies. More than a millennia ago, Chinese emperors fastened their robes with buckles carved from the casque of the sacred hornbill and restored themselves with soup made from swallows' nests gathered in a land so strange that tales brought back to China were scarcely believed.

An Arab voyager, Ibn Batuta, sailing past North Borneo in the mid-14th century, gave the world its first description of Mount Kinabalu (and, incidentally, of the edge of a typhoon). Referring to "the great Mountain of Clouds", he went on to say: "at the foot of the mountain arise black clouds accompanied by winds which rise up the sea and wreck all that is found on that sea".

Pigafetta, who accompanied Magellan's fleet on the first circumnavigation of the world, visited the Muslim Sultanate of Brunei in 1521. He spoke of the carpets, silks, porcelain and brass canon adorning the Sultan's palace, but even more wondrous were the trees "making leaves which, when they fall, are alive and walk". Pigafetta's introduction to the brilliantly disguised leaf insects of the rainforest had him totally fooled.

By the 19th century, there were stories of head-hunting tribes; of impenetrable jungles filled with apes so resembling humans they were called "man of the forest" (orang-utan), and of swashbuckling traders

Murut tribesmen c. 1909 (courtesy Sabah State Museum)

Kota Kinabalu, capital of Sabah

who could either become a White Rajah or see their settlements burned to the ground by marauding pirates.

The world's third largest island was believed to be a vast, jungle-covered land where untold riches lay. Indeed, the old name for the island still used in the Indonesian portion, Kalimantan, means "river of precious stones"; the name Borneo is a Western corruption of Brunei. A huge lake was believed to exist on the south side of "Mount Kinny Baloo", a lake "so large that the land is not visible across it". (Maps drawn even as late as the beginning of this century persisted in showing this non-existent lake, the subject of ancient legends.)

Men were living in North Borneo as long as 31,000 years ago; today's tribes, however, are believed to be descended from Mongoloid settlers who arrived in about 3,000 BC. The land in which they lived was, since at least the 12th century AD, under the nominal control of the Sultan of Brunei. The north and northeastern portions of Borneo eventually came under the sway of the nearby Muslim Sultan of Sulu, in what is now the southern Philippines.

Such matters as political control were supremely irrelevant to the scattered communities existing on fish and starch produced from the sago palm in coastal regions, or hunting wild game and gathering the abundant fruits and other edible jungle plants in the almost inaccessible interior.

Stilt village near Sabah State Mosque

Buying Borneo

Towards the end of the 19th century, during the height of the colonial expansion throughout Southeast Asia, Borneo inevitably attracted the attention of a number of Western powers: the Americans, Italians, Spanish, Austrians, British and Dutch, the latter two already being established in the Malay peninsula and much of Indonesia. North Borneo eventually went to an Austrian, Baron Von Overbeck, who acquired rights from the Sultans of Brunei and Sulu. In 1881, in partnership with Englishman Alfred Dent, he set up a company to administer the territory. They obtained a Royal Charter and a year later, the British North Borneo Chartered Company came into being and Von Overbeck bowed out of the picture.

From the very beginning of Chartered Company days, the settlement of North Borneo was run as a business, bringing tremendous changes to the land and its people. The Company set about quelling piracy, planting tobacco, developing rubber estates and importing Indonesian and Chinese labourers to work in them. Bridle paths linking the various settlements were cleared, the telegraph introduced, and work begun on the proposed Trans Borneo Railway that was intended to link the east and west coasts. To finance all this, the Company demanded that taxes be paid by the natives.

This so incensed the son of a Bajao chief, Mat Salleh, that he formed a rebel army and in 1897, totally destroyed the British settlement on Gaya, the island opposite today's Kota Kinabalu. He eventually retreated inland, building a fort in Tambunan where he was besieged and finally killed by the British in 1900.

Mat Salleh and his men weren't the only ones to resent the intrusion of the British. The isolated Muruts, dwelling to the far southwest, felt their traditional lifestyle was threatened and rose up in 1915 in Rundum. This revolt was mercilessly quelled by the British, who somehow manhandled a cannon over impossible terrain to slaughter around 400 rebels.

The capital of North Borneo was established on the east coast in Sandakan (after its first couple of years in the northern settlement of Kudat). After the destruction of Gaya, the main west coast settlement was moved to the site chosen as the terminus for the Trans Borneo Railway. This narrow strip of land, with the hills on one side and the sea on the other, was named Jesselton after a director of the Chartered Company. Owing to the shortage of land, most native housing was perched on stilts over the sea; vestiges of these *kampung air* (water villages) remain even today, despite frequent reclamation pushing the water's edge further and further away.

In the first few decades of Company rule, North Borneo produced an adequate return from its rubber, although its mineral wealth (copper, silver, gold and oil) remained undiscovered. The jungle continued to provide its traditional riches – rattan, wild honey and wax, *damar* (a resin), rare bezoar stones and rhinoceros horns (both erroneously believed to have medicinal value).

Modern Times

North Borneo suffered badly during the Japanese occupation of World War II and the Allied bombing that forced their surrender. The capital, Sandakan, was totally demolished, while in the town of Jesselton, just three buildings were left standing. In 1946, the capital was transferred to Jesselton, while North Borneo itself was handed across to the British Crown. Unable to finance the enormous cost of reconstruction, the Chartered Company bowed out and North Borneo became a colony.

In 1963, after a series of discussions in which it was agreed that the two British colonies in Borneo (North Borneo and Sarawak), would retain a certain amount of autonomy, the Federation of Malaysia came into being. This linked the Malay peninsular states once known as Malaya with nearby Singapore (which quit the Federation two years later) and Sabah and Sarawak, separated from mainland Malaysia by several hundred kilometres of sea.

North Borneo was renamed Sabah, the name which the locals had always called their country, but whose meaning no one seems able to agree upon. There was no mystery, however, about the new name for the capital when the colonial Jesselton gave way to Kota (City) Kinabalu.

Hand in Hand

An early visitor to North Borneo remarked that "the diversity of peoples, the countless languages, dialects and sub-dialects used have all made the people more tolerant." Sabah is Malaysia's most diverse state, where the easy going tolerance of the past still exists.

Among its population of around 1½ million, there are at least 30 different ethnic groups, the biggest being the Kadazan/Dusuns, who form around 30 per cent of the population. The Kadazans are in reality a collection of many different groups with at least 10 distinct languages, although they are linked by similar cultural beliefs. Traditionally rice farmers, they dwell on the coastal plains, the slopes of Mount Kinabalu and the rich coastal valleys in the interior. The majority of the Kadazan/Dusun are now Christians, although some old beliefs are retained and in certain communities, priestesses still conduct age-old ceremonies to ensure a propitious harvest.

Yayasan Sabah building, KK

The coastal folk, long exposed to contact with the outside world, are mostly Muslim. On the east coast in particular, they lived in their boats (always ready for a spot of piracy) until encouraged on shore by the British North Borneo Company. Even today, many of the coastal fishermen remain poised between land and sea, living in houses perched on stilts at the water's edge.

The biggest coastal group, the Bajaos, originated several centuries ago in the southern tip of the Malay peninsula and migrated to the Sulu region, eventually coming south to Sabah. They have adapted to the land with a vengeance in the past century, becoming renowned buffalo farmers and horsemen, particularly in the Kota Belud region. The Suluk and Illanun are also from the southern Philippines, while the coastal Muslim Kadazans are known as Idahans or Orang Sungei; there are also smaller groups of Visayans, Bruneians and Malays.

The most remote people are the tribes who were forced further and further inland by later settlers. These tribes – the Rungus living in northwest, and the Murut, Lundayeh and Kelabit dwelling south towards the borders of Kalimantan and Sarawak – are the last to cling to traditional lifestyles. Few of them, however, still hunt with blowpipes, and communal dwelling in longhouses is slowly dying away. Most of the Muruts and Rungus have exchanged animism for Christianity, and with the younger generation exposed to education and modern lifestyles, the traditional ways are inevitably fading.

It is a stunning experience to see a group of Sabahans on a festive occasion, when they change their everyday Western clothing for their distinctive traditional dress: Murut men aquiver with pheasant feathers and clad in beaten bark cloth; Suluk girls looking like Oriental princesses in glittering golden headdresses and shimmering silk; Kadazans in black edged with gold and wrapped with belts of silver coins; Rungus women a-jingle with tiny bells, draped with antique beads and intricately woven cloth, and Bajao men in gaily beaded and embroidered jackets and trousers, their folded headdress set at a rakish angle. On such occasions, the rich diversity of Sabah's people is immediately apparent.

The Latest Wave

The cultural potpourri of North Borneo was further enriched by the Chinese, brought in by the British in the early 1880s. The first group were Cantonese from Hong Kong, mostly shopkeepers who found no demand for their skills in the new settlement. The next batch were hard-working Hakka farmers, all Christians from the Basel Church in southern China, who proved such successful immigrants that the trend continued, making the Hakkas the biggest single Chinese group found today in Sabah. Uniquely in Southeast Asia, roughly half of Sabah's Chinese population are rural workers, as opposed to traders and shopkeepers in the towns. Today, the Chinese community forms the second biggest ethnic group in Sabah. Over the years, many Chinese have intermarried with locals, particularly the Kadazan/Dusun, further adding to the almost bewildering ethnic mix.

Indonesian labourers from nearby Sulawesi, Flores and Timor, flocked in to join the workforce several decades ago, joined more recently by other Indonesians who labour in the oil palm, cocoa and rubber estates. Filipinos fleeing the conflict between the Muslim Mindanao and the Philippine government arrived en masse during the 1970s when they were given safe haven by the State Government. They have been joined since then by thousands of illegal economic migrants whose presence is a problem yet to be solved.

Many Paths to God

Most visitors are surprised to learn that, unlike Peninsular Malaysia, Sabah is not a predominantly Muslim state, although Islam is the official religion as in the rest of the Federation. The majority of Sabahans are Christian, with Muslims forming the second biggest group. Mosques, churches, Buddhist, Taoist, Sikh and Hindu temples and Bah'ai meeting halls all exist to meet the religious needs of Sabah's diverse people.

Economy

The first recorded export of timber from British North Borneo was in 1885, when a slump in world prices encouraged a sugar plantation owner near Sandakan to almost literally cut his losses by felling his trees. It wasn't until almost a century later, in the 1970s, that Sabah's rich rainforest was fully exploited, and for the past couple of decades, timber has provided the State government's major source of revenue (33 per cent in 1989).

In dollar terms, Sabah's most valuable export in recent years has been crude petroleum, which is found offshore. But because Sabah keeps only 5 per cent of the revenue earned by petroleum exports, this potentially valuable contribution to the state's coffers is less important that its other major exports, palm oil and cocoa.

To slow down the rate of logging and to expand local manufacturing, there has been a shift away from exporting whole logs towards processed timber, such as sawn wood, plywood and furniture. Such changes require sawmills, factories and the availability of skilled labour, all of which are in short supply in Sabah. Meantime, the State Government is searching for ways to continue logging on a sustainable basis, so that the rainforest, of immeasurable value both to Sabah and the whole world, will not be destroyed forever.

As experts look to reforestation, planting of fast-growing softwoods, and using the forest for traditional resources such as rattan and medicines, others see an increasing interest in nature tourism (or, to use the current buzzword, "ecotourism") as the answer to preserving Sabah's forests. Whatever the future may bring, today's visitor to Sabah still has the rare opportunity of being able to enjoy the amazing beauty and diversity of the rainforest in a world where this precious and fragile environment is fast disappearing.

HISTORICAL HIGHLIGHTS

AD 700-1400: Chinese annals record early trade between the Celestial Empire and the coastal settlements of north Borneo, including the Sultanate of Brunei.

1521: Magellan's fleet visited Brunei, an event which is recorded as the first contact between Westerners and the people of Borneo.

1577: The Spanish colonised the Philippines and brought the Sultanate of Sulu under their nominal control.

1662-74: As a result of wars of succession in Brunei, the Sultan of Sulu was promised the area that is now Sabah by Muhuideen, who failed to honour his promise on becoming Sultan.

1761: The British East India Company entered into an agreement with the Sultan of Sulu and founded a trading post on the island of Balembangan, near Kudat. The settlement, named Felicia, was not a success and was burnt to the ground by pirates in 1775.

1764: The Sultan of Sulu ceded all of North Borneo, including Labuan, Banggi and Balembangan islands, to the British East India Company.

1846: The Sultan of Brunei ceded Labuan island off the west coast of Sabah to the British Crown.

1865: The American Trading Company established the settlement of Ellena in Kimanis (southwest Sabah), after obtaining a 10-year lease from the Sultan of Brunei. The settlement failed after a year.

1875: The lease to Kimanis was sold to Baron Von Overbeck, who renewed it for another 10 years.

1877: Overbeck joined forces with the Dent brothers of London and signed new leases with the Sultan of Brunei for a larger territory, as well as leasing land from the Sultan of Sulu.

1881: Dent signed all his rights to North Borneo (including those already transferred to him by Overbeck) to a company which was granted a royal charter. Kudat became the first capital of British North Borneo, while trading posts were established on Gaya Island and Sandakan.

1882: The British North Borneo Chartered Company was officially formed, and in the following three years, bought more land in North Borneo.

1884: Sandakan, which had first been settled at Kampung German in 1878 and was resettled a year later as Elopura, became the capital of British North Borneo.

1894-1900: Mat Salleh, a Bajao chief, constantly rebelled against the British presence, razing Gaya in 1897, until he was finally killed in a siege.

1896: Work was begun on the proposed Trans Borneo railroad.

1899: Jesselton was founded on the mainland opposite Gaya and flourished as the railroad took shape.

1942: Japanese forces occupied Sabah.

1946: The capital was moved from Sandakan to Jesselton owing to the total destruction of Sandakan during Allied bombing raids at the end of the war. Sabah became a British Crown Colony as the Chartered Company could not afford to rebuild the war-devastated country.

1963: North Borneo became independent and reverted to its pre-colonial name, Sabah, on becoming the 13th state of the Federation of Malaysia.

1967: Jesselton, originally named after a director of the North Borneo Company, was renamed Kota Kinabalu.

1985: Sabah became the first state in Malaysia to elect a non-Muslim State Government, run by the Kadazan Christian-dominated Parti Bersatu Sabah.

Activities

Many of Sabah's attractions require a minimum of one day to visit, and those who want to enjoy it to the full will need at least two or three days (or more) to travel to and explore more remote locations such as the virgin rainforest of Danum Valley, Sipadan Island's marine wonders, the Turtle Islands off Sandakan, and to climb to the summit of Mount Kinabalu.

From your base in the capital, Kota Kinabalu, you can make a series of half-day or day trips to explore the town, its nearby islands and fishing villages; to discover the rich beauty of Sabah's rare plant life; to go white-water rafting or stroll the nature trails on Mount Kinabalu before moving further afield.

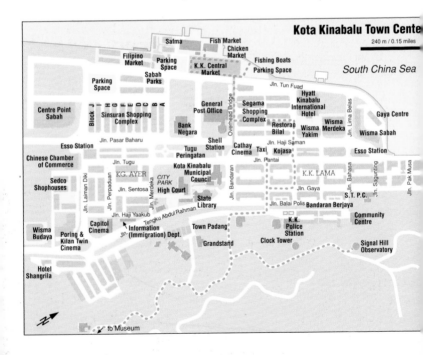

Kota Kinabalu Town Centre

240 m / 0.15 miles

A jumble of produce at KK market

Half-Day Trips

Morning Market, Museum, Mosque and Munchies

Feel the pulse of Kota Kinabalu, with an early morning prowl through the Central Market followed by a pause for a somewhat theatrical breakfast. After the panoramic view from Signal Hill, the Museum (closed on Friday) introduces the rich diversity of Sabah. View the impressive State Mosque en route for lunch.

Start before breakfast around 7.30-8 am at the north end of the Central Market and walk past the car park to the waterfront for a view of the huge, brightly painted fishing boats. Across the channel you can see the stilt villages of Gaya Island perched over the sea, home to several thousand Filipinos.

Enter the market at the back door facing the car park; this will bring you to a couple of stalls selling soya bean milk and delicious warm soya bean junket (*tau foo fa*). For M50 cents, the vendor will scoop it from a huge stainless steel drum into a bowl, then pour on sugar syrup. Sit on a nearby bench and enjoy.

Suitably restored, you can now wander through the market, where you'll find everything from fresh fern tips to imported grapes, orchid plants to porcelain tea cups. Take your time and you may spot sellers of basketware, see strings of what look like huge white beads (dried yeast for making rice wine), smell the fragrance of countless fresh herbs, local tobacco, areca nut and betel leaf and discover the Aladdin's cave where the tang of spices mingles with the aroma of freshly ground local coffee.

All this amazing food is sure to have given

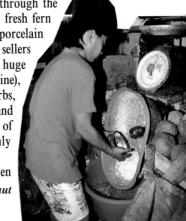

Instant grated coconut

you an appetite. Climb the stairs at the north end of the market near where you came in and take the pedestrian bridge; later in the day, this is an excellent place to spot colourful characters selling traditional medicines, Rungus beadwork, wild honey and the like. Take the third exit to the left from the bridge and walk down into the Segama shopping complex. Pass the old Chinese men chatting at the base of the steps and continue down until you see Restoran Bilal, on your right. Order a couple of *roti canai* and watch the performance of the Indian cook as he swings out a ball of dough in ever-increasing circles to create the lightest, flakiest pancake you've ever eaten.

Continue down the pedestrian mall, past Restoran Ali where even at this hour, crowds of men are glued to the video screen where American wrestlers strut their stuff, and turn right into Jalan Datuk Salleh Sulong. Continue across busy Tun Abdul Razak, across Jalan Pantai (once the waterfront of KK) and turn right at the quaint old Chinese liquor-cum-fabric store into Jalan Gaya, the heart of old KK. Walk down a block, taking time to gaze into the Chinese grocery stores where goods dangle from the rafters, spill out from the shelves and occupy almost every inch of floor space.

The row of shophouses on the opposite side of Jalan Gaya were the first to be constructed, in 1951, after World War II decimated KK. Look up on the hillock nearby and you'll see one of the three structures to escape bomb damage, the quaint old clock tower built in 1905 in memory of the town's first district officer, who died of "Borneo fever" at the age of 28. As late as 1956, the lights of the clock tower were used as navigational aids by local shipping; today, the tower is completely obscured by surrounding buildings.

Turn right from Jalan Gaya and take a taxi from the nearby rank. Ask the driver to take you up to Signal Hill to the observation point, then on via Jalan Istana to the Museum – not the quickest but certainly the most picturesque route which should cost from M$8-10. The taxi will pass the Padang, an open green where the colonial British first played cricket in 1901, then turn left up Signal Hill (Bukit Bendera), climbing up to the Observatory where you can gaze down over the town, catch sight of the orange-roofed Tanjung Aru Resort to the far south, and spot the dozens of reefs playing artist with the sea, painting it jade, azure and turquoise.

Sabah State Museum

Jalan Istana cuts through a tunnel of greenery along the ridge of exclusive Signal Hill, passing fine old bungalows tucked almost out of sight and the Istana (Palace), residence of the Head of State. Shortly after,

Imposing Sabah State Mosque

you'll approach the Sabah State Museum. Do not go straight into the main building, but turn right across the car park and into the display of life-sized traditional houses (open at 10 am), arguably the most interesting section of the entire museum. Here you can wander about the longhouses and other homes of Sabah's major tribes, peep into the kitchens full of typical cooking implements, look at the various tools and fishing traps and notice the herbs, vegetables and medicinal plants in the gardens outside.

It's time now for the main body of the museum. The ground floor has an interesting ethnography section on the left, particularly the costumes, while to the right, the historical photos of KK are worth a close look. At the back on this side is a reproduction of a cave, complete with swallows' nests and the paraphernalia used to gather this precious commodity. The natural history display on the right side of the 1st floor is small but interesting.

As you come out of the museum, pass the old locomotive and take the steep path down through the palm trees to the main road. You'll see the State Mosque just ahead of you. Walk closer and have a look at the beautifully proportioned domes and minaret, the golden Arabic characters swooping like birds over the soft grey stone. The interior of the mosque is somewhat disappointing, so skip this and start considering lunch.

If you fancy hot stuff in cool surroundings, take a bus in front of the mosque and go a couple of stops to Komplex Kuasa. Walk behind this brown tile complex, across the street to the centre known as Sadong Jaya. Set back about a block, near several other restaurants, you'll find the semi-open air Restoran Kampung Air, with a small airconditioned dining room. (Do not confuse it with the

Old Clock Tower

Kampung Restaurant). They have a wide selection of good, moderately priced Malay food, to which you can help yourself, as well as a range of Asian and Western dishes featuring locally grown rabbit. Unusually for a restaurant serving Malay food, beer is available. (For other lunchtime options, see "Eating Out")

Lazing and Lunching on a Tropical Isle

Swim in crystal clear waters, exploring the wonders of the coral reef; laze on a talcum-powder beach as hornbills fly overhead, and wander the nature trails of Sapi or Gaya Island – all this literally minutes from downtown Kota Kinabalu.

You can do this trip either in the morning or afternoon, bearing in mind mornings are more predictable in terms of fine weather; try to avoid Sunday, when the islands are busy with local visitors. First of all, have your hotel pack you a picnic lunch or, better still if you're staying in town, go to Tong Hing Supermarket at the top of Jalan Gaya (open 8 am) for fruit, cheese, cold cuts, savoury buns or sandwiches and drinks. Ask the butchery section to let you have a chunk of ice to keep it all cool.

Take a taxi (M$8) or a bus to the Tanjung Aru Resort; if going by taxi, ask the driver to follow the Coastal Highway, which will

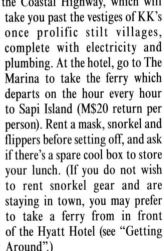

take you past the vestiges of KK's once prolific stilt villages, complete with electricity and plumbing. At the hotel, go to The Marina to take the ferry which departs on the hour every hour to Sapi Island (M$20 return per person). Rent a mask, snorkel and flippers before setting off, and ask if there's a spare cool box to store your lunch. (If you do not wish to rent snorkel gear and are staying in town, you may prefer to take a ferry from in front of the Hyatt Hotel (see "Getting Around".)

The ferry will take about 20 minutes to bring you to Sapi, a pretty little island joined at low tide by a sand bar with the biggest of the Tunku Abdul Rahman Park islands, Gaya. (The Park, administered by Sabah Parks, is a protected area, so please do not take any shells, coral or plants.)

Beach in Tunku Abdul Rahman Park

Underwater coral garden

Find a shady spot, a picnic table, and enjoy relaxing and swimming in the amazingly clear water; you'll notice a dramatic change in water colour as the shallow reef drops off abruptly to a depth of 18 metres.

The best coral is off the southeast tip of the island (Gaya is roughly to your north). If you're not a snorkelling enthusiast, you can use the Sabah Parks' glass-bottom boat for a trip over the reef. This service is readily available every Sunday, and other times by prior arrangement; phone Sabah Parks (211585, 211881, 212719, 211652) a day in advance to request the glass-bottom boat. Alternatively, you may be able to persuade the ranger in charge on Sapi to do the trip for you (M$4 per person).

You'll see dozens of brilliant fish in a kaleidoscope of colours: turquoise, blue and pink parrot fish, neon blue guppies, cheekily striped clown fish and lemon-yellow angel fish. The reefs themselves, although sadly destroyed in some areas, have a rich diversity of corals in all shapes, sizes and colours, together with waving fronds of weeds and sponges.

Well-marked trails permit you to walk around Sapi. Watch out for the black and white pied hornbills, quite often seen flying between Sapi and Gaya. You can swim or wade across to Gaya and take the 40-minute hike along the trail to the boardwalk through the mangrove forest near Camp Bay (the old Park Headquarters). Look closely at the mangrove forest, where you can often spot kingfishers, crabs and mud-skipper fish that seem as home on land as in the sea.

If you're returning late afternoon, walk along the sea wall in front of the Tanjung Aru Resort and along the beach to the food stalls (about 10 minutes), then refresh yourself with the juice of a young green coconut and maybe an ear of freshly boiled sweet corn while waiting for the spectacular sunset (between 6-6.30 pm, depending on the time of year).

Morning Trail Ride and Handicraft Hunt

If you've ever sat on a horse, this is all the skill you'll need to go on a 2-hour trail ride through lovely rural scenery complete with lush padi fields, split bamboo houses, birds and butterflies. Cool off on a beach-front verandah then head back to town for a little souvenir hunting.

Call Dale Sinidol, tel: 225525, a day in advance to arrange to be collected at around 6.30 am for the trip to Kinarut Riding School. The scenery near the beachside stables doesn't prepare you for the remarkably pretty rural valleys and gentle hills you'll be exploring this morning.

Comfortably astride your pony, you pass through Kinarut village, a quaint cluster of big old wooden shophouses. The road narrows and soon you're onto a country lane, shaded by giant stands of bamboo and fruit trees. Dozens of birds provide a melodious accompaniment to your ride. Watch for butterflies, too, especially as you follow the stream.

Split bamboo houses float in a sea of emerald padi fields which lap at the feet of the hills. "*Kuda, kuda*! (horse)", kids shriek delightedly. Sarong-clad women wading the water-logged fields with a fishing net pause to smile, while back home, hens and piglets search the backyard under mango or breadfruit trees. It's difficult to think of a nicer way to see, hear, smell and feel the countryside than at a gentle walk on horseback.

After your return to the stables, ask Dale to take you to Seaside Traveller's Inn just down the road. Sit on the upstairs verandah in the breeze for a panoramic view of the beach and islands as you enjoy a drink. Look at bizarrely beautiful hornbills in cages to the left just as you're leaving the Inn.

Padi fields near Kinarut village

Tempting goodies at Filipino market

When you get back to your hotel, you'll probably want to take a quick shower and change before going on to the Filipino Market, on Jalan Tun Fuad Stephens opposite Sabah Parks' office. The market is a huddle of wooden stalls separated by a maze of narrow alleys. Although many of the stalls seem to be selling the same curtains of shells, cascading macrame hangings, woven baskets, wood carvings and sunhats, look a little closer and you may find some original and attractive items. Be sure to bargain; you may get as much as one-third off the original asking price. Apart from Filipino favourites, there are several stalls selling Indonesian batik fabric, Iban baskets from Sarawak, and local Sabahan pottery (mostly the glazed, incised variety). Among the glittering stones (frankly fake) you may find genuine Sabah pearls, though if you want to be sure, shop at a jewellers (try Wisma Merdeka or Centrepoint).

Walk up past the main market and take the pedestrian bridge that leads to the Post Office. The bridge should be filling up with hawkers offering bottles of wild honey, folk medicines, cheap trinkets and toiletries. Blind musicians tend to hang out here, and you can often spot a group of Rungus tribespeople. The most traditional women wear brass bangles and antique beads as they sit barefoot in black home-spun sarongs, stringing cheap bright beads into necklaces and bracelets. Their menfolk, often wearing a folded headcloth or *dastar*, squat over piles of tobacco.

Go to the far end of the bridge, turn left down the stairs, and you're back in the main street of town. You might like to walk up the road a couple of hundred metres to Wisma Merdeka, where there are a couple of shops specialising in Sabahan items (see "Shopping"), then cross to Wisma Sabah where there's yet another gift shop to tempt you. By this time, you'll be ready to head back for your hotel or to go to lunch.

Day Trips

A Tale of Two Cultures

Two contrasting communities – the Bajaos in a traditional fishing village of thatched houses perched above the water, and the rice-growing Dusuns living in an idyllic valley – are both within easy reach of Kota Kinabalu. Visit a pottery factory en route, and finish with a picnic and swim in the river.

You'll need to hire a car for today's trip. Pack a picnic lunch and swimming gear, and set off around 8 am if possible to avoid the hottest part of the day while you're exploring the fishing village. Drive north along Tuaran Road, which leads through the industrial area of Inanam, past Menggatal to Telipok village. After you've passed Telipok, watch on your left for the sign "Tuaran 9 km"; a few hundred metres beyond, on the left, you'll see the Soon Yii Seng pottery, where visitors are welcome and prices more competitive than in downtown KK.

For centuries, Chinese ceramics have been an important trade item in Borneo and antique jars are treated as priceless heirlooms. Traditional styles such as huge jars with embossed dragons are still created at Soon Yii Seng, while other classical Chinese shapes are incised or embossed with Sabahan and Chinese motifs. Although many items are now made in moulds, you can still see men throwing pots on a wheel, and women painstakingly doing the detailed finishing work and decoration.

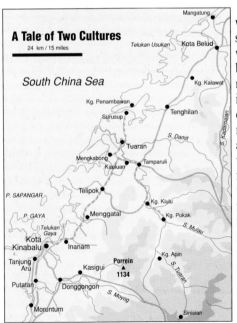

Just follow the signs towards Tuaran, going straight at the roundabout where the road to Kinabalu Park branches to the right. Suddenly, the semi-industrial sprawl of KK's outskirts is replaced by rural scenery as picturesque as you'll find anywhere, with padi fields, water buffalo, simple wooden cottages, a lush tangle of fruits trees, palms and flowering shrubs. All this is framed against – if you're lucky – the dramatic backdrop of 4,101-metre Mount Kinabalu.

When you reach Tuaran

Standard transport at Kampung Penambawan

town, pass the clock tower in the centre of the divided road, veer slightly to the right and continue along the narrower, two-way road which leads past the Police Station, over an old bridge spanning the Tuaran River and on towards Kampung Surusup. Continue straight along this road, ignoring the few side tracks that lead off it, until you come to the end of the road at the river's edge in Surusup, about 10-15 minutes beyond Tuaran.

Park your car and ask at the little store on the right for Haji Abdul Saman, who is happy to take visitors upriver by boat to the Bajao fishing village, Kampung Penambawan, for around M$10. If you are prepared to pay M$30-$40 for an hour, he'll also take you to the river mouth (*kuala*), an incredibly pretty spot where the river and sea merge with sandbars, pristine beaches and shady casuarina trees – take your pick and either swim in the surf or bathe in the river.

As you turn a bend about 10 minutes upriver from Surusup, Kampung Penambawan floats into view, an Asian Venice where dozens of *attap* (palm-thatch) houses linked by walkways cluster at the edge of the wide river. I find it hard to understand why this particular fishing village – less than an hour by road and boat from Kota Kinabalu – should have escaped the less attractive aspects of "civilisation". You won't see any TV aerials,

Drying fish

Typical suspension bridge

plastic junk floating in the water or rusting corrugated iron roofs here. I must confess to feeling somewhat ambivalent about encouraging you to visit Penambawan, and can only plead that you'll respect the privacy of the folk here. Do not walk into homes without an invitation, and ask before photographing women and older folk (the kids'll be pleading for photos!). As you explore, watch out for the pottery jars used for storing fresh water, women weaving mats from pandanus leaf, split fish or bananas drying in the sun, and folk paddling along in dugout canoes from house to house. You won't miss the dozens of cats who do very well on a diet of fresh fish. The river provides a bounty of crabs and prawns as well as fish, a ready source of income for the fishermen of Kampung Penambawan.

The Bajaos, who originated in the southern tip of the Malay peninsula, came to Sabah via the Philippines. It might occur to you as you teeter for balance on some of the more precarious *nibong* palm walkways, that it's a good thing that the Bajaos are Muslim and therefore forbidden to drink alcohol; negotiating the walkways in a less than sober condition is a challenge I'd hate to face.

Leave the Bajaos behind and retrace your steps to Tuaran. When you come to the highway at the roundabout, take the A1 towards Tamparuli, Tawau and Sandakan. Just before Tamparuli, a blue signboard on the left indicates a right turn to Tamparuli. Turn right and continue for a couple of minutes until you pass the substantial white hilltop headquarters of the Seventh Day Adventist Church. Turn right at the narrow, unmarked road to Kiulu, just before the

Washday at Kampung Pukak

bridge crossing the river in front of Tamparuli. Follow this often steep, winding road for 15-20 minutes until you see a fairly substantial village on the river to your left. The road forks just before a bridge; take the left fork over the bridge towards Kiulu (there is no signpost). Continue driving on the main road, passing Kiulu and a large school to the left (with the sign "Selamat Datang") and take the road marked "Jalan Pukak". You'll know you're on the correct road when you pass the big mosque a moment or so later.

You're now well and truly in Dusun territory, the land of the hill-farming Kadazan/Dusun tribe, hardy folk who have, for generations, planted rice in these rich valleys and on the lower slopes of the Crocker Range. For the next 10-15 minutes, you drive through glorious scenery with terraced paddy fields, simple farmhouses, giant stands of bamboo, glimpses of the river burbling over smooth stones and spanned by suspension bridges seemingly as frail as a spider's web.

At Pukak, a cluster of rough wooden stalls and shops on both sides of the road, take the left-hand fork of the road downhill towards the school ("Sekolah Kebangsaan Pukak, Tuaran") and follow a hairpin bend to the left. Continue down this dirt road for a couple of hundred metres and you'll suddenly find yourself in a wide grassy field at the edge of the river, the opposite bank a wall of green rearing up almost vertically. To the left, you'll see a suspension bridge and a small wooden hut. Take time to try the suspension bridge, which is remarkably strong despite its often alarming swaying motion.

To reach one of Sabah's most gorgeous picnic and camping sites, drive carefully upriver along the flat green field for about 200 metres where, out of sight of the village and shaded by trees and bamboo, you can revel in the beauty of the surroundings. A little upriver, there are rapids where you can let yourself be excitingly whirled down by the current (depending on the amount of water), or you can swim in the deep, clean stretch of river that forms a respite before the next rapid. You may even see a rubber dinghy float by as a group of tourists enjoy a rafting trip down the Kiulu River, becoming popular for its combination of beauty and relative ease of navigation.

When you can eventually bear to tear yourself away, follow the same route back, turning left as you come off Jalan Kiulu. From here the way back to KK (about 1½ hours from Kampung Pukak) is clearly signposted.

(You might like to stay overnight at the Pantai Dalit Rest House (see "Where to Stay"), just 20 km from the roundabout where you turn off to Tuaran; the road to Pantai Dalit is clearly sign-posted.)

Mountain Meandering

Spend the day among what one expert described as "the richest and most remarkable assemblage of plants in the world" around Park Headquarters on Mount Kinabalu. Join a guided nature walk, look for pitcher plants and orchids in the Mountain Garden, and stroll through the forest along a mountain stream, all in spring-like temperatures at 1,500 metres.

Rhododendron javanicum

Travel to Kinabalu Park by mini-bus (about 2 hours and M$8), leaving from in front of the KK Padang, or go by shared taxi leaving from the same area (M$15 per person). There's also a bus (M$5) leaving for Ranau near the Padang at 8 am daily, passing the Park. Try to leave no later than 8 am, and bring field glasses (if possible), comfortable footwear and a light jacket.

The route to the mountain takes you through industrial Inanam and past Telipok, a pottery centre. Just as the the padi fields and water buffalo of Tuaran district come into view, the road swings right; watch on the left for suspension bridges as you near Tamparuli village. The road now begins its winding climb. Try to sit on the left of the bus for views of terraced gardens carved out of the steep hillsides, and for tantalising glimpses of the summit of Mount Kinabalu and the waterfall.

Nabalu market, about 15 minutes before Park Headquarters, is known for its durian and *tarap* fruit, green and red-skinned bananas,

Mount Kinabalu

hill rice and wild honey; you can also pick up a typical Kadazan hat or *sompoton* (musical instrument) for half the city price. On market day (Thursdays), the place is thronged with sturdy Dusun women hefting over-loaded woven back packs (*wakid*).

The mini-bus will take you right up to the entrance of the Kinabalu Park (M$2 for day visitors). Have a look at the gift shop and maybe buy one of the very informative, inexpensive publications produced by Sabah Parks to enhance your visit. Wander down to the Kinabalu Balsam restaurant and relax over a drink on the verandah with a good view of the mountain (clouds permitting) and a chorus of birdsong; Mount Kinabalu has around 280 species of birds, some of them found nowhere else in the world.

Kinabalu Park encompasses a variety of habitats, ranging from lower montane forest around Poring (about 550 metres) to montane and upper montane forest, with the harsh granite slabs leading to the summit (4,101 metres) denying all but the hardiest forms of life. The summit, often covered by clouds which sweep up with tremendous speed, can re-appear just as suddenly. This dramatic peep-show makes its series of jagged peaks all the more awesome when they thrust into view (one feels such an occurrence should be accompanied by a melodramatic drum roll).

Walk down the road to the Administration Building, enjoying the treeferns and mountain oaks; behind this three-storied building you'll find the Mountain Garden, where the labelled collection of plants serves as an excellent introduction to Kinabalu's flora. Watch out particularly for orchids (many of them tiny), pitcher plants and rhododendrons. Take the marked trail across the stream, pausing to read the notices and to listen to the sounds of the forest.

Pitcher plant

Map labels

South China Sea — Kota Kinabalu ★ — SABAH — MALAYSIA — SARAWAK — Kuching — KALIMANTAN — Samarinda — Pontianak — Balipapan — INDONESIA — Banjarmasin

Mount Kinabalu
1600 m / 1 mile — Victoria Pk. 4094 — Lows Pk. 4101 — Pond — Ugly — Lows Gully — Donkeys Ears 4054 — St. Johns Pk. 4096 — Sister Pk. 4032 — Mushroom Pk. — Sayat Sayat Hut — Kinabalu South 3932 — Tunku Abdul Rahman Pk. 3948 — Panar Laban Rockface — Gunting Lagadan Hostel — Burlington House — Panar Laban Huts — New Hut — Laban Rata Resthouse — Shelter — Paka Cave — Helipad — Shelter — Shelter Lipsan's Trig — Bypass

400 m / 0.25 miles — Power Station — Kiau Gap — Mempening Trail — Silau Silau Trail — Kombongoh Trail — Liwagu Trail — Cave — Twin Bed Cabins — Nepenthes Villas — Admin. Bldg. — Bukit Tupai — B. Tupai Trail — Liwagu Cave — Kiau View Trail — Cabins — Hostels — Bukit Burong — Silau Silau Trail — B. Burong Trail — Cave — Restaurant Headquarters — Bukit Ular — Liwagu Trail — Helipad — Bundu Tuhan Trail — to Ranau

Helipad — Shelter — Radio Sabah Transmiter TV Complex — Layang-Layang — Shelter — Kambarangoh Telecoms Station — Cascade Waterfall — Shelter — Carsons Falls — P.W.D. Power Station — Shelter — Liwagu — Helipad — Park Headquarters

You should be back in front of the Administration Building by 11.15 am for the guided nature walk, led by one of the Park staff. If there are a lot of visitors, the group walk can become a little frustrating; try to be as close to the guide as possible so you can hear clearly and ask any questions.

You'll be happy to know that the food in the Administration Building restaurant is very good indeed. After the guided walk, why not try Chinese or Malay cuisine, with some mountain-grown vegetables such as "sweet beans" (green peas cooked in the pod). After lunch, go upstairs to the exhibit centre for historical pictures and miscellaneous information on Mount Kinabalu. You might like to relax in one of the armchairs in the lounge before setting out for a hike through the forest.

There are a number of marked trails, but perhaps the prettiest (and easiest) is the Silau-Silau Trail, heading towards the Power Station Road and not Liwagu Cave. Walk down past the Mountain Garden and along the road to the sign "Bukit Tupai Trail". Walk down a few metres; don't turn left where you see the small suspension bridge but go right for about 5 metres and just before the bridge leading to the sports hall, turn left and go downhill across the river. At the sign "Bukit Tupai Trail, Silau-Silau Trail 4 mins., Bukit Tupai Shelter 15 mins", turn left for the Silau-Silau Trail, which meanders through the forest in company with the sparkling Silau-Silau River.

As you walk, watch out for butterflies, including the famous black and iridescent green Rajah Brooke's Birdwing; you'll probably see tree shrews and squirrels, though spotting the birds you'll hear singing is often more challenging. Look closely at the vegetation, for many of the orchids, fungi and other plants are minute, as are most of the frogs and insects. The majority of trees at this altitude are oaks, chestnuts and laurels, although there are also clusters of thorny rattan palms.

Where the Silau-Silau Trail comes out to the Power Station Road, you can either return the way you came, or spend about another hour coming back along the Kiau View Trail; reach this by crossing the Power Station Road and walking down until you see the signpost on your right. This trail, which offers a number of fine viewpoints looking over hillside villages, eventually comes back onto the road near Park Headquarters.

Leave the Park no later than 4 pm, and walk down to the main road to wait for a passing mini-bus or taxi to take you back to Kota Kinabalu.

Riding the River

As you hurtle blindly through a torrent of water crashing around jagged rocks, you may wonder why you decided to go white-water rafting on the Padas. But if you love excitement, a chance to view the rainforest from tranquil stretches of river, with a ride on a quaint railcar thrown in, don't miss this trip, one of the high points of any visit to Sabah.

The only feasible way to go rafting on the Padas River is to organise your trip through a tour operator. Api Tours (tel: 218829), whose adventure travel specialist, Jon Rees, pioneered white-water rafting in Sabah, is still the best operator. Provided the river level is not affected by a dry spell in the interior, Api Tours will collect you at your hotel around 6 am for the drive to Beaufort. Bring a change of clothes, sunscreen and a pair of gloves if possible. During the 1½ hour bus trip, you'll have ample opportunity to enjoy the picturesque rural scenery and occasional glimpses of the coast.

At Beaufort, after loading the special inflatable raft onto the railcar, there's time for breakfast in the old wooden shophouses facing the station. They're built high on stilts to avoid the periodic flooding of the Padas – one even has a canoe ready under the porch! Go to Christopher's Corner Parking on the end if you want a Western breakfast (and an exceptionally clean toilet), or have Chinese noodles or *dim sum* at Chung Mei.

Note the chainsaw carried on board by your railcar driver: Borneo still produces challenges even along well-travelled routes. The stretch of railway between Beaufort and Tenom, completed in 1905, was the only link (apart from tracks) between the west coast and the agriculturally rich interior until as recently as twenty years ago.

Fun on the Padas River

Preparing the raft

You'll be riding the railcar for about an hour to your launching point which is further up the Padas River.

The toytown railcar, which seats just 13, rattles past isolated hamlets and gardens worked by Murut tribespeople as it follows the lower reaches of the Padas River, rather tame at this point. As the gorge narrows and cultivation gives way to the rainforest, the river, which drains most of the interior of southwest Sabah, protests at its constriction. Walls of water rear up against huge boulders, or form a tumble of chaotic waves as they race across rapids. Gazing at the river from the safety of the railcar as your guide explains the quirks of each rapid and how you're going to negotiate it, you may well have second thoughts about the whole venture.

Too late. You've arrived at the launching point and are already being given instructions on how to paddle the raft. Donning your crash helmet and safety jacket, you join other rafters for a trial run and learn how to cope should you fall out of the raft. Despite the challenging nature of the Padas in full flood, even novices under the competent guidance of Api Tour's experts can run the rapids quite safely.

Finally you're off, and depending upon the state of the river, you'll spend the next 2 to 4 hours rafting down to the station where you've already left your lunch and dry clothing. Heart-pounding rapids alternate with tranquil stretches where the beautiful forest, a darting kingfisher and a dugout canoe pulled up on the bank compete for your attention.

As your raft nears the finishing point and the river decides it's finished its show of fury, it's time to let yourself fall overboard (something you've been trying to avoid all morning) and take a swim in the refreshingly cool water. Your lunch tastes amazingly good after the excitement of the river, and the trip back to Kota Kinabalu seems remarkably tame after the wild Padas. You can be sure you'll sleep well tonight!

Going Ape in Sandakan

It's hard to believe that in just one day (albeit a long one), you can fall in love with the adorable orang-utans in the Sepilok sanctuary, thread through the maze of mangrove forest at the edge of Sandakan Bay, then drift along the Kinabatangan River to see Borneo's unique proboscis monkeys in the wild.

Before leaving Kota Kinabalu, you'll need to arrange with a tour

Swamp forest in eastern Sabah

company for your afternoon trip to the Kinabatangan, with a transfer to Sandakan airport for your return flight. Time is tight, so you must have this confirmed in advance. You may prefer to have your tour operator handle all arrangements for the entire day. However, it is less expensive and very easy to go by taxi from Sandakan airport to Sepilok by taxi, remaining independent until meeting your tour operator for your trip to the Kinabatangan. (Api Tours are recommended for their knowledgeable guides.) Bring field glasses if possible, as well as sunscreen and a hat for your afternoon boat trip. Try to buy a copy of the small but tremendously informative book, *Orang-utan: Malaysia's Mascot* (see "Further Reading") before leaving for Sepilok.

It's an early start this morning, to catch the 6 am flight to Sandakan. Sit on the left side of the plane for a dramatic view of Mount Kinabalu. Gazing down at the heavily forested mountains and, as you approach the east coast, the thick swamp forest with its snaking brown rivers, you can understand why most of Borneo remains untamed.

When you arrive at Sandakan, arrange for a taxi for the 20-minute trip to Sepilok Orang-utan Rehabilitation Centre (about $25), to arrive by 9.30 am at the latest, then ask the driver to wait while you have breakfast upstairs at the airport restaurant. Set in 43 sq. km. of virgin

Playful babies

Learning the ropes at Sepilok

forest just 25 km from Sandakan, the Sepilok sanctuary was begun in 1964 to help motherless baby orang-utans, usually caught in logging operations, learn to live in the wild. Sabah's Wildlife Department permits visitors to Sepilok to observe the twice-daily feeding in an effort to promote an interest in conservation.

Before you enter the reserve, you'll have the opportunity to photograph and even fondle one of the two orang-utans who have shown a marked preference for human company and refuse to go wild. They are brought out to "meet the visitors", as handling orang-utans inside the reserve is strictly forbidden to avoid spreading disease. The most intelligent of apes, the orang-utan (found only in Borneo and Sumatra) is astonishingly human in its behaviour, gentle, curious, playful and altogether irresistible.

Follow the rangers along the short walk to the first feeding platform where orang-utans still learning to adjust to the forest are given their twice-daily ration of bananas and milk. After this first feeding, the rangers move on to a second feeding platform deeper within the forest, where the orang-utans are more independent. There's a very steep, often slippery hill to climb, so this second platform is only advisable if you're wearing proper footwear and are moderately fit. Should you decide to go, you'll be able to enjoy the beautiful forest as you walk.

Feeding time

When you've satisfied your desire to watch the adorable orang-utans, have a look at the small display centre, and also see if the shy rhinoceros is out of his stall and taking a wallow.

Take a bus from just outside the sanctuary into Sandakan town, where you can enjoy lunch before meeting your tour operator for the trip up the Kinabatangan River. You might like to try Chinese food in the airconditioned restaurant upstairs at the Sandakan Recreation Club, at the back of the town Padang (green), just a 5-minute walk from the bus station. Although the Club is for members only, the 1st floor SRC Restaurant is open to the public.

After meeting your tour operator around 2 pm, you'll cross Sandakan Bay by speedboat, with a chance to look back at the town that was Sabah's capital until 1946, and which is an important centre for oil palm, timber and seafood. Soon, you'll be threading your way through salt-water mangrove forest. Look at the boardwalks and fishing boats of Kampung Mamiang before turning into the mouth the the Kinabatangan, Sabah's biggest river. Watch for the change in vegetation as you leave the salt-water for fresh-water swamp; the mangroves become diversified, with the *Sonneratia* variety favoured by the proboscis monkey interspersed with *nipahs* and other beautiful palms. As you motor upriver, you should see white egrets, kingfishers and broadbills, although from about 4 pm onwards, your eyes will be peeled for the groups of monkeys which come down to feed at the river's edge as the day gets cooler.

Rare rhino

The proboscis monkey, found only in Borneo, is a droll creature once described as "the grotesque honker of the Borneo swamps". With a nose Jimmy Durante would envy, a pot belly and a mixture of grey and red fur, the male looks like he's wearing tights and a jacket he's outgrown. He flings himself with insane abandon from one tree to the next, crash-landing noisily, and is altogether the most entertaining monkey you could come across. The much smaller females have a more refined appearance with delicately uptilted noses, and are far less exhibitionist in their behaviour.

You can be certain of seeing several groups (up to 20 is not unusual), as well as numbers of macaques which often feed near the proboscis monkey, as you go slowly upriver to the village of Abai, then turn back towards Sandakan for your eventual return to Kota Kinabalu.

Rafflesia bloom

Overnight

On the Nature Trail

See the world's biggest flower, picnic and swim amidst a cloud of butterflies, then explore a remarkable collection of rare Borneo orchids and wander about a living museum. Stay overnight in Tenom, riding the quaint railcar along the dramatic Padas Gorge to return to Kota Kinabalu next day.

You'll need to arrange either for a hire car with driver, or for a taxi (around M$200) to take you to Tenom and stay with you until around 5.30 pm. Before leaving KK, call Tenom Railway Station (087-735514) to book your seats on the 7 am railcar from Tenom to Beaufort the following morning. Also, advise the Agricultural Research Station in Tenom (087-735661) that you intend visiting the Orchid Centre around 3 pm. Pack swimming gear, mosquito repellent and a picnic lunch (or plan to buy food en route) and leave KK around 8.30 am.

Your first destination is the Rafflesia Information Centre in the rainforest of the Crocker Range. After passing through Penampang, the road begins its steep climb up sharply ridged mountains, a never-ending sea of green waves flowing down to the coast. Beyond Kampung Moyog, look to the left for glimpses of Mount Kinabalu. Fresh *shiitake* mushrooms are grown in the thatch huts by the road, while isolated farmers raise pineapples, bananas and vegetables which they sell in simple roadside stalls.

About an hour after leaving KK, you'll come to Gunong Emas motel and restaurant, where it's time to stop for coffee and a concert provided by caged *shamas*, Asia's most melodious songbird. Keep hunger at bay with a few *woh teh*, excellent light pork-filled dumplings prepared by an elderly Chinese lady famous for this speciality.

As you travel on towards the Sinsuron Pass,

which crosses the range at 1,649 metres, watch out on your right for views down to Kota Kinabalu and the islands dotted off the coastline. Within 10 minutes, you should reach the Rafflesia Information Centre (on the left), which contains all you could possibly wish to know about the amazing flower discovered by Sir Stamford Raffles in Sumatra. A parasitic plant whose bloom can grow up to one metre in diameter, the Rafflesia's life cycle takes a whole 9 months or more. A ranger at the Centre, which opens at 10 am daily, will be able to tell you where to see Rafflesias in bloom along the reserve's trails. Take just a few minutes to follow the Lookout Trail to the shelter overlooking Sinsuron on the Tambunan plain below. The altitude of around 1,000 metres makes hiking very pleasant; watch out for orchids on trees and fallen branches.

Continue down the road to Tambunan where, if you haven't packed a picnic lunch, you can buy cooked Chinese food from Restoran Tambunan next to Sabah Bank. Keep heading south along the highway until the marked turn-off to Bingkor, just before Keningau. At Bingkor's cluster of old wooden shophouses, turn right towards Taman Bandukan, a delightful pic-

Sinsuron lookout

nic spot by a river renowned for its thousands of butterflies. Pause here for lunch and a splash in the stream, and don't be surprised if butterflies land on you. You'll need to leave at 2 pm at the latest to arrive by 3 pm at the Tenom Orchid Centre.

Go on through Keningau to Tenom, an attractive town in a rich agricultural region where Muruts are the predominant ethnic group. Turn left just before the Padang (open green), cross the railway line and head for the Agricultural Research Station (often incorrectly called the Cocoa Research Station) some 20 km away. The guard will let you in when you advise you have already phoned for permission to visit.

At the Orchid Centre, suitably armed against mosquitoes, you can wander about Borneo's

Rare native orchid

biggest collection (around 500 species) of native orchids, plus many other interesting blooms from around the world. (Borneo contains about 2,500 or 10 per cent of the world's total known species). See if you can find, among the many rare and un-usual flowers, the bloom that smells of raspberry jam, the Mexican orchid which produces the vanilla pod and a small orchid whose hinged lip snaps shut with surprising strength to trap unwary in-sects. The orchids range in size from tiny pin heads to cascades of blooms several metres long.

If time permits, go to the nearby Crop Museum, where dozens of plants and trees are grouped according to their use (medicines, bev-erages, oil, perfume etc). There are plans to make this living muse-um part of a full-scale Agricultural Park in the near future, and with informative booklets and guides available, this will offer an exceptional chance to learn more about the myriad of plants essen-tial to mankind.

Head back for Tenom, where you part company with your taxi or hire car to spend the night (see "Where to Stay"). For dinner, try the YNL Entertainment Centre's restaurant just across the Padas River (5 minutes by taxi); their steamed tilapia, a fresh-water fish raised locally, is excellent. There's a karaoke lounge at YNL, a chance to see how the locals enjoy a night out.

Necklace orchid

Next morning, try to be at the railway sta-tion by 6.40 am to get a seat in front of the railcar, or on the left hand side, for the best view. The railway, until recently Tenom's on-ly link with the coast, cuts through a narrow gorge as it follows the Padas River, Sabah's best for white-water rafting. Early morning is the loveliest time to ride the railcar. The rising mist is caught in the forest canopy and the spiders' webs strung with diamonds of dew. Birds greet the new day with ec-static calls, some of them swooping across the river in search of insects. Other ear-ly birds – children en route for school – join the railcar for a short ride down to the dis-trict school.

When you arrive at Beaufort Station around 1½ hours later, cross to the old shophouses opposite for breakfast. Christopher's (on the corner) has wholesome bacon and eggs and other Western food, while Chinese breakfast of *dim sum* or noodles is the way to start the day at Chung Mei.

Take either a mini-bus (M$5) or share a taxi (M$8 per person) for the 1½ hour trip back to KK.

Traipsing in the Treetops

Get a monkey's-eye view from a walkway strung high in the jungle canopy, soak in hot springs, hike to a waterfall and dream with the butterflies during a day at Poring, part of Kinabalu Park. After a night in the mountain cool, revel in the amazingly diverse plant life around Park Headquarters before returning to KK.

As there is no regular transport service between Poring and Kinabalu Park Headquarters it's easiest to either hire a car for two days, or charter a taxi to stay with you until evening the first day (you can return by mini-bus the following day). Spend the evening in the Kinabalu Park (It is essential to book accommodation in advance; see "Where to Stay"). Pack a swimming costume and towel for the hot springs and leave by about 7.30 am for Ranau. (Avoid doing this trip on a Sunday, when Poring is extremely busy with local visitors.)

Follow the route up to Mount Kinabalu (described in "Mountain Meandering"). About 5 km on past the entrance to Kinabalu Park, you'll see the important agricultural district of Kundasang; a clutter of ramshackle stalls offers a delectable range of mountain produce, a drawcard for locals who like to stock up on vegetables direct from the garden.

Kundasang is also home to a war memorial honouring both local civilians and armed forces who died during the Japanese Occupation. In Ranau, a much more simple memorial (a cairn of stones

Canopy walkway at Poring

Death March memorial at Ranau

topped by a green-painted helmet) was erected by the Australian Armed Forces, in memory of the almost 2,400 prisoners of war who died on a march from Sandakan during the final days of the Japanese Occupation (there were just 6 survivors).

When you reach Ranau, you can buy food for lunch (only cold drinks are available at Poring Hot Springs, although there are future plans for a restaurant). Restoran Sin Mui Mui, in the street parallel with the main road and at the back of the Ranau shopping area, will pack you a lunch box; choose from their wide range of ready-cooked Chinese and Malaysian dishes, including tasty chicken curry, and you can buy some fresh fruit at the nearby market.

Follow the signs for Poring Hot Springs (Air Panas), 27 km along a sealed road from Ranau. At Poring, located in the eastern part of Kinabalu Park, there's an entrance fee of M$2. First plan should be to go the canopy walkway, which opens at 10.30 am and costs $2 per head. (Between 4.30 pm-10.30 pm, the charge is M$30 for a group of 3; from 10.30 pm-10.30 am, it's M$60.) It's about a 30-minute walk, across a suspension bridge, past the rock pool and hot baths and up a steep hill to the three massive trees which anchor the walkway.

The first of its kind in the region not restricted to scientific use, Poring's walkway, suspended high in the forest canopy, provides the perfect position for viewing the ephiphytes clinging to the huge

Refreshing Rock Pool

Maiden's Veil fungus

dipterocarp trees. There are some spectacular views down to the forest floor and across the valley. Sitting quietly high in the trees, you get a close-up look at the birds, squirrels, tree shrews and, at night, flying lemurs and other nocturnal creatures. Watch out especially for the handsome black and orange Prevost Squirrel.

When you return from the walkway, relax in a tub of hot mineral water. The baths, originally built during the Japanese occupation, were designed for utility rather than aesthetics, but the glorious surroundings – stands of enormous *Poring* bamboo which gives this area its name, hibiscus, fruit trees, palms and even pine trees – more than compensate. When you're thoroughly relaxed, pluck up courage and plunge into the cold water of the beautifully landscaped rock pool. (Oh, that the hot pools were similarly designed! The new enclosed baths are also attractive, and one can only hope that eventually the old baths will be replaced.)

Decide how to spend your afternoon: there are several marked trails you can follow (most fairly steep), to waterfalls and to a tumble of boulders where bats spend the day hanging upside down. If you feel energetic, take the 1½ hour trek to the lovely Langanan Waterfall; since few visitors come here, you're more likely to see wildlife such as monkeys and deer, although orang-utan and bear are now virtually non-existent in the Park.

You might decide to concentrate on butterflies and the iridescent dragonflies which can be seen around the hot baths or trickles of mineral-rich water nearby. A butterfly park, like a huge aviary where you can

Butterfly Park resident

observe hundreds of live butterflies, has recently opened. Filled with brilliant flowers and even more brilliant butterflies, the Taman Kupu Kupu has at least 30 species from the Poring region; one of the most spectacular is the vivid yellow and black Common Birdwing. Butterflies are most active during bright sunlight; if it's cloudy, just wait for the sun (and the butterflies) to reappear.

Drive to Kinabalu Park Headquarters for a relaxing night in beautiful surroundings, with the fresh mountain air to give you an appetite. The restaurant in the Park's Administration Building offers a range of good local as well as Western food. For a very different view of the forest, go for a night walk with a good torch along one of the trails. Look closely on and under leaves for stick insects, ranging from about 4 cm up to a giant 30 cm; where you might also spot luminous fungi and some of the tiny frogs common to Kinabalu.

Get up early in the morning for a walk along the roads near Headquarters to spot the hundreds of birds intent on awakening the whole world. (Their songs can be taken back home in the form of a cassette tape, "Kinabalu Chorus", sold at the Park's gift shop.) Breathe in bracing mountain air over breakfast on the verandah of the Kinabalu Balsam Restaurant (near the Park entrance) then wander down to the Mountain Garden for an introduction to the flora of the Park. Watch out particularly for the carnivorous pitcher plants, whose leaves are adapted into a cup where hapless insects are digested. If you're lucky, the rare slipper orchid may be in bloom.

If you're not in a hurry, stroll along one of the nature trails (see Itinerary #5 for a description of the Silau-Silau Trail) before driving or catching a mini-bus from outside Headquarters back to town.

Birds & Beasts

See caves where birds' nests that pleased the palates of Chinese emperors are still gathered, then drift through the swamp forest for an intimate close-up of the outrageous proboscis monkey and a rainbow of birds. After a night on the banks of the Kinabatangan River, cross Sandakan Bay to return to Kota Kinabalu.

Sandakan city and bay

It is possible (though very time-consuming) to travel to Gomantong Caves independently. (Take the 11 am boat from in front of Sandakan market to Suan Lamba for M$3, then hire a local car for about M$60 to travel to and from the caves; the return boat doesn't leave until 5 am the next day.) However, exploring the Menanggol River by boat and spending the night in comfortable accommodation on the Kinabatangan is feasible only by taking an arranged tour. (Contact Api Tours, (088)-221233 or Wildlife Expeditions, (089)-219616.)

You're up with the birds to take the 6 am flight from KK to Sandakan; ask for a window seat on the left of the plane when checking in for dramatic views of Mount Kinabalu and of the swamp forests around Sandakan. When you arrive, ask your guide to take you to the coffee shops near Sandakan market for breakfast; Hap Shing has excellent Coto Makassar, a beefy soup with chunks of rice cake. You'll probably have time before your boat leaves to visit Sandakan market; buy some fruit for your trip, and explore Sabah's biggest and most interesting fish market.

As you leave by speedboat from near the main mosque, you have a clear view of the town, wedged into the narrow strip of land between steep hills and the sea. When the British took over North Borneo, there were just three villages in the vast Sandakan Bay, one of them a base for gun-runners supplying Sulu. Since most of those involved in the smuggling were German, this was known as "Kampong German". Somewhat fortuitously, this was burnt down and a new settlement named Elopura (Beautiful City) rose up on the site of today's town, eventually reverting to its old Sulu name, Sandakan ("The Place Which was Pawned").

Sandakan is the centre of Sabah's forestry industry; you can still see ships loaded with huge logs heading out across the bay. Before

Gomantong Caves

long, you're passing fishing boats trawling for prawns and fish, catch a glimpse of tranquil stilt villages fringing the islands, then arrive at the jetty and cluster of houses comprising the village of Suan Lamba. From here, it's 4-wheel drive territory as you set off through a huge palm oil estate towards Gomantong Caves.

The final approach to the caves is a disused logging track through land that is a sad shadow of its former beauty, with a tangle of secondary growth rather than the magnificence of primary rainforest. You know the caves aren't far away when you come across a row of make-shift food stalls catering to the workers who harvest the birds' nests.

Harvesting is strictly controlled by the Wildlife Department to

Swallows' nests

avoid excessive exploitation. Twice a year, for a period of about 2 weeks, workers risk their lives to
climb flexible rattan ladders dangling from the
cave ceiling, then inch along bamboo ladders to
reach the nests stuck to the roof, as much as 60
metres above the floor of the cave. The harvesting season varies from year to year, with
March to May, and September to November
being the periods in which the nests are generally taken. Although a visit is obviously
more spectacular during harvesting, at any time of year
the caves are impressive.

Two varieties of swiftlet make edible nests in the caves: those
where the saliva is mixed with feathers are found in the so-called
"black" cave, which may be visited, while the more expensive nests
of pure saliva are found in the less accessible "white" cave. Bats also frequent the caves, which are carpeted with a thick layer of guano
housing thousands of beetles and other insects. Definitely a place
for sensible footwear!

As you pause for a picnic lunch near the entrance to the caves,
watch out for birds attracted by the nearby stream and flowering
shrubs. Then it's time for an hour-long drive to village of Sukau,
on the banks of Sabah's biggest river, the Kinabatangan. The boat
trip to the lodge where you'll spend the evening takes all of 2 minutes. One of the nicest aspects of this big wooden house is the shel-
tered verandah overlooking the river. The beds are tempting, too,
so rest until around 3.30 pm when it's time to set off up a tribu-
tary of the Kinabatangan, the Menanggol River.

As you motor slowly up the narrow river, it's like being in a tiny
country lane after the highway of the Kinabatang. You're an in-
separable part of the environment, sur-
rounded by mangroves and other swamp
forest, within intimate distance of an Oriental Darter which knifes into the water
beside you, or a mangrove snake coiled in
the branches just a metre or so overhead.
The birds along the Menanggol are simply stunning. With the *"Pocket Guide to
the Birds of Borneo"*, you'll be able to
identify the hornbills noisily flapping overhead, the Storkbilled Kingfisher with
gleaming enamelled blue wings, the dra-
matically beautiful ruby and jet Broadbill
with his pale blue beak and whiskers and
the exquisite Asian Paradise Flycatcher
with its trailing tail feathers. If you're not
already a confirmed birdwatcher, be pre-

Nest gatherer

47

pared to be converted by this matchless display of feathered beauty. It is an experience to be savoured.

As the day cools, the proboscis monkeys come down to the river to stoke up for the night on their favourite *Sonneratia* leaves. Thanks to the quiet isolation of the Menanggol, the monkeys seem remarkably unconcerned as you approach, stop the engine, and gaze at their antics. The height of the trees is lower than along the Kinabatangan, allowing you to see the monkeys from a remarkably short distance. If you come across a mixed family group, you can see a mother anxiously protecting her baby, and giant pot-bellied old males who gaze down their pendulous noses with a look of disdain before opening their legs to display yet another prominent part of their anatomy (they're renowned exhibitionists!). Young males scrape with each other like kids, then leap with more bravado than skill into another tree.

Only the falling of night can persuade you to leave such an enchanted wilderness. Back at your lodge, a delicious meal awaits, then the promise of a cool night watching the river. Maybe there'll be fireflies, or a tug towing rafts of felled logs that extend herringbone fashion as much as 300 metres behind. Comfortably protected by mosquito netting from the moths and bugs of the night, you'll sleep well until awakened the next morning by birdsong. After early breakfast, it's time to drive back to Suan Lamba then cross

the bay to Sandakan, just 1½ hours but an entire world away.

You can return to Kota Kinabalu today, or you might have organised this trip to include an extension to Selingan, one of the islands where the turtles come to lay their eggs. If you have time before catching your flight, take a taxi to the Forestry Department (Ibu Pejabat Perhutanan) to see the interesting exhibit centre. The past and present of forestry, Sabah's most important industry, is attractively presented, together with samples of the various woods found here. Don't miss the ironwood pile that was part of Sandakan's jetty for 50 years and still looks like new. The exhibition centre is open during normal government office hours and is free.

Proboscis monkey

48

Laying green turtle

Turtles Galore

Experience conservation in action at remote Pulau Selingan as you watch the Green Turtle dragging herself ashore at night to lay her eggs. When the protected eggs are hatched, the baby turtles are carefully returned to the sea, something which you can assist in if you don't mind the tiny creatures scrabbling all over your feet as they race for the ocean.

To reach Pulau Selingan, 1½ hours off the east coast town of Sandakan, you can make arrangements with a tour operator in Kota Kinabalu or phone boat owner K.T. Tan, tel: (089) 42878. Because of the distance involved, transport is not cheap but seeing the turtles is a priceless experience. You must book accommodation in advance in the comfortable Sabah Parks' chalets (tel: (089) 273453). The best time to visit is between April and October, when the largest number of turtles is to be seen and the southwest monsoon makes the voyage by sea more comfortable. Bring a swimming costume, sunscreen, insect repellent and torch with you.

Leave Kota Kinabalu on the 6 am flight, making sure you request a window seat on the left side of the plane for the best views. On arrival at Sandakan, if you're not being met by a tour operator, take a taxi to the bus station beside Sandakan market (about M$15-18) and have breakfast in one of the coffee shops or Indian Muslim restaurants opposite. You might like to buy some fruit and snacks in the market, as the restaurant on Pulau Selingan is limited and naturally more expensive. Travel by taxi (M$2-3) to the jetty where you've arranged to meet your boat.

The boat trip should take between 1 to 1½ hours, depending on the state of the sea. You'll pass the nearby island of Berhala, once a leper colony and then a prisoner-of-war camp. The coastline is eventually left behind as you head towards the three "Turtle Islands", Selingan, Bakungan Kecil and Gulisan, purchased by the state government in 1971 to ensure their status as sanctuaries. Poaching of the eggs (which fetch around M$1 each in the market) was a problem for many years, compounded by the proximity of the Philippine islands. To protect the turtles and their eggs, armed po-

Hatchlings at Turtle Island

Racing for the sea

lice reinforce the Sabah Park rangers by patrolling the islands. Sadly unaware of international boundaries and differing attitudes towards conservation, turtles also lay their eggs on the Philippine islands nearby, eggs which can often be found on sale in Sandakan market.

When you arrive at Selingan, you'll have the rest of the day to swim in the beautifully clear water, to walk around the island (a 30-minute exercise) or just relax. After watching the sunset, have a look at the hatchery, where baby turtles should now be emerging in the evening cool from the sand into a netted enclosure, after a gestation period of 50-60 days.

After dinner, wait in your chalet for a ranger to call you when the turtles are coming up the beach to lay their eggs. It is vital not to disturb the turtle with bright lights or noise, so crouch quietly in the warm night as you watch a huge shape drag herself laboriously up the beach to begin digging a pit with her flippers. She pauses frequently to give an almost human sigh before continuing her exhausting task. When the pit is ready, she squats over it and begins to drop 100 or more eggs, a stream of soft-shelled ping-pong balls. As she begins to cover the eggs, the ranger will tag her then lift her to one side, scooping the eggs into a bucket, then return the turtle who persists in covering the pit before dragging herself back to the sea.

Follow the ranger back to the hatchery where he'll bury the newly laid eggs, tagging the spot with a marker indicating the date and number of eggs. Then it's time to carry the hatchlings that have just emerged from the sand into their protected enclosure

Incubating eggs

down to the water's edge. If you ask, the ranger will let you help in this exciting task, but be warned: as you tip the baby turtles out of the bucket on to the sand, they tickle like crazy as they run over your feet, scattering in all directions before being guided by a torch beam and some deep instinct into the sea.

During the height of the laying season, more than a dozen turtles may drag themselves onto the beaches of Pulau Selingan during the course of an evening. Each time, the rangers repeat their performance, gathering and re-burying the eggs in the hatchery. It is estimated that only 30 per cent of the baby turtles released into the sea survive to adulthood. By some still unexplained phenomenon, female turtles, on maturity, will return to the very beach where they themselves were hatched to lay their eggs.

You'll return to Sandakan following an early breakfast. You may wish to follow another itinerary – a trip up the Kinabatangan to view the proboscis monkey, returning to KK on the last flight, for example, or visiting Sepilok for the 2.30 pm feeding of the orang-utans – before flying back to KK.

Three- to Five-Day Trips

Climbing To The Top of Borneo

All of north Borneo lies at your feet as you triumphantly stand on Low's Peak, 4,101 metres above the waters of the South China Sea. The highest peak between New Guinea and the Himalayas, Mount Kinabalu is a magnet that no visitor in good physical con-

Laban Rata rest house

The summit at last

dition should resist.

Many climbers attempt the trip from Kota Kinabalu to the summit and back in just 2 days. It can, of course, be done (the fastest man up to the summit and back to Headquarters did it in less than 3 hours!), but why push yourself so hard that you haven't time to enjoy the beauty of the mountain and feel so exhausted that the rest of your stay in Sabah is spoiled? You are strongly urged to spend one day acclimatising around Park Headquarters (1,500 metres), climbing at a leisurely pace on the second day to accommodation at Panar Laban (3,352 metres). On the third day, you make for the summit, returning to Park Headquarters and then back down to Kota Kinabalu or perhaps spend a night at Poring hot springs.

Book your accommodation in advance at Sabah Parks (see "Where to Stay"). Before leaving Kota Kinabalu, make sure you have warm clothing; the temperature can fall below zero on the summit. Trainers are preferable to heavy boots, and a change of socks should be brought as the track is often wet. Gloves are essential for grasping the ropes on the granite slopes; so, too, is a torch. A light plastic raincoat or poncho can be useful, and many climbers swear an umbrella is indispensable. You will not need to carry water on the first day, as it's available at every rest point; however, a ½ litre plastic bottle of water for drinking on the summit is recommended. Chocolate and biscuits can be bought at Kinabalu Balsam Restaurant at Headquarters; if you want apples and nuts, buy them before leaving KK. Headache tablets to cope with any discomfort caused by the altitude are also recommended.

It is commonly claimed that Mount Kinabalu is one of the world's easiest mountains to climb. True, it doesn't require any mountaineering skills, and the well maintained trail follows the line of least resistance on the way up. But make no mistake: the climb is extremely strenuous, taxing both your legs and lungs. If you're planning an ascent well in advance, it's worth jogging regularly to get yourself fit.

Ever onwards and upwards

So there you are, all packed and raring to go. If you're carrying a heavy pack, you may find the Ranau bus, which departs at 8 am from near the north end of the Padang, gives you more room. Otherwise, take one of the Ranau mini-buses in front of the Padang for the 2-hour, M$8 trip to Kinabalu Park.

Register when you arrive at the Park then spend the rest of the day familiarising yourself with the mountain. Check the exhibit centre on the 1st floor of the Administration Building for interesting historical and botanical information, and aerial photos of the mountain. You'll learn that geologically speaking, Mount Kinabalu is a mere babe, its summit shaped by the last ice age 10,000 years ago, and still growing. You'll also discover that the mountain is host to species of plants, birds and small animals found nowhere else in the world.

Visit the Mountain Garden for a taste of what you're likely to encounter as you climb, for the mountain offers such strikingly different plants as rattan and rhododendron, bamboo and buttercups, orchids and oaks,

pitcher plants and violets. You might like to join the guided nature walk starting in front of the Administration Building at 11.15 am. You could also explore one of the marked trails around Headquarters, though don't overdo it – you're going to need all your energy tomorrow.

On Day Two, be sure to be at the office just inside the Park entrance by 7 am to pay for your climbing permit (M$10) and obtain a compulsory guide (M$50 for 2 days for 1-3 persons). If you are particularly interested in the flora of the park, ask for a specialist guide. Take a pick-up or Park bus (M$10 per person) to the Power Station (otherwise a 1-hour walk) where you begin your climb. The earlier you start, the better, as weather conditions often deteriorate in the afternoon.

As you leave the lower montane forest, you'll notice changes in the vegetation as you enter a dense, cool kingdom where thick moss drips from the trees, and where climbing bamboos and tree-ferns crowd together. At each rest stop, don't miss the interesting information panels. Some of the 25 species of rhododendron found on the mountain may be in bloom in the high level moss forest; watch out for the spectacular golden *Rhododendron lowii*, or the orange *javanicum*. At around 2,700 metres, a change in soil causes a dramatic difference, with much more open vegetation which is home to the pitcher plants (*Nepenthes*). Around 3,000 metres (and getting closer to the end of today's climb) the trees seem to shrink, their tortured limbs twisted by the wind.

By the time Laban Rata Rest House comes into view, you'll be able to gaze at the uncompromising granite bulk of the summit looming above you, its harsh stone slabs denying life to all but the most tenacious plants clinging to tiny pockets of soil. Enjoy your well-earned rest, a good meal, and maybe even a doze before wandering down to the helipad for a view of the sunset (weather permitting).

Your guide will try to persuade you to get up at 2 am for an early breakfast and a 3 am departure for the summit. The combination of food and high altitude makes many people feel nauseous, so lim-

Carnivorous pitcher plant

it yourself to a hot drink and take chocolate, nuts and fruit (not forgetting your water) to the summit. The guides are convinced that every climber has a burning desire to see the sunrise from the summit. If you don't mind pulling yourself by rope up a granite rock face while trying to hold your torch in the dark, freezing in the pre-dawn cold, then queueing up with other climbers to stand on the summit, follow the guide's advice. Or do as I do, and leave at 5 am so that by the time you're scaling the first granite face, you no longer need a torch and have both hands free for the rope. You'll be warmed by the rising sun as you reach the most exposed portion of the mountain, which can be bitterly cold before dawn. As you finally approach Low's Peak (2 hours from Laban Rata), all the other climbers are on their way down and you'll have the summit to yourself.

The first man to reach this peak (in 1888) was botanist John Whitehead, naming it after Hugh Low who climbed the mountain in 1851 but, owing to a broken altimeter, failed to find the true summit. On a clear day, the view from this tiny peak is stunning, as the forested hills, rivers, estuaries and coastline lay sprawled far below. Equally breathtaking is the 1,800 metre chasm of Low's Gully, which virtually splits the mountain in two. When you can finally tear yourself away from the view, retrace your steps to the Rest House, have breakfast and a rest before going back down to Park Headquarters.

You can purchase a certificate to prove you've made the summit, though your aching legs are going to remind you of the fact constantly over the next 2 or 3 days. Take a mini-bus back to KK

Kinabalu's highest growing orchids

or, if you can spare another day, go on to Poring Hot Springs (see "Traipsing in the Treetops") to treat yourself to a soak in the hot tubs. Stay overnight in one of the hostels or chalets; remember to buy food in Ranau en route. Be sure to arrange with the mini-bus or taxi which brought you to Poring to pick you up the following day to return to the city.

Treasures of the Deep

Dive with turtles, moray eels and shoals of shimmering fish in pristine waters around Sipadan, Malaysia's only oceanic isle rising 600 metres from the floor of the Celebes Sea. Awesome walls of coral, undersea caverns and teeming marine life make this one of the world's best dive spots.

For maximum enjoyment of Sipadan, you should be a certified scuba diver; without proof of certification, you will be limited to snorkelling the waters over the reef. If you have the time, you can do a dive course in Kota Kinabalu before travelling to Sipadan. Before flying from KK to Tawau, you must arrange your trip with a dive operator (Borneo Divers are strongly recommended: see "Sports"). A place described by Jacques Cousteau as "an untouched piece of art" and as having "more marine life than any other spot on the face of this planet" (by WWF) demands a minimum of 3 days, preferably 4-5.

You'll leave on the early morning flight to Tawau, on Sabah's east coast. After breakfast, there's a drive by mini-bus through endless palm oil and cocoa plantations to Semporna, nestling on the southeast tip of the huge Darvel Bay. Long the haunt of Bajao sea gypsies, most of Semporna keeps one foot in the sea with its fishing villages high on stilts above the somewhat murky water.

From Semporna, it's about 1½ hours by fast local boat until the tiny dot on the horizon turns into a tree-covered island surrounded by brilliant white sand. Your eyes are abruptly pulled from the sim-

Approaching Sipadan Island

Sipadan's waters teem with turtles

ple wood and thatch huts of Borneo Divers' Sipadan Dive Lodge by the changing colours of the sea. Deepest indigo turns abruptly to jade green as the limestone pinnacle on which the island perches mushrooms out.

Until recently, Sipadan Island was visited only by nesting Green Turtles and birds (many of them migratory). Despite the construction of limited accommodation for divers, the island retains its pristine quality. As for the underwater world, all you need do is don your gear and go. Your first dive, under the supervision of a divemaster, is done off the beach in front of the Dive Lodge. Swim just a few metres from the water's edge and you're above a sheer wall of brilliant corals plunging vertically downwards as if to the very centre of the earth, offering uncomparable wall diving.

Over the next few days, you'll be able to do unlimited diving to discover the varied wonders of Sipadan. There's the awesome Turtle Cavern, a network of caves some 20 metres underwater where skeletal remains indicate that some of these creatures, perhaps losing their bearings, met their end in a watery grave. Far happier will be the inevitable encounters you'll make with live turtles each time you dive, as they swim fearlessly about you.

The fear might be coming the other way when you dive Whitetip Avenue, a shelf where Whitetip Sharks bask on the sand some 10 metres or so underwater, or when you witness a maelstrom of silver as a huge shoal of barracuda flashes past. After just one dive, the astonishing number and variety of fish surrounding Sipadan, not to mention the profusion of corals in every colour and shape imaginable, plus sea whips, anemones, fan worms and sponges, will convince you that the Great Creator saved up all his artistry

Fun at Borneo Divers

Segama River in Danum rainforest.

and imagination for the underwater world.

The world above ground is thoroughly satisfying too, as you live the simple life barefoot in the sand. The most important creature comforts are amply catered for. The beds are comfortable and mosquito-netted, and the unroofed showers let you admire orchids and epiphytes festooning shady trees while getting clean. Your three meals a day are excellent, with plenty of fish and tropical fruit to remind you where you are. Diversions such as the late afternoon volleyball game between the staff and guests, games of Trivial Pursuit, songs around a guitar and swapping of dive stories make you wonder why anyone ever bothers with TV.

An alternative night entertainment is watching the turtles coming ashore to lay their eggs, something which occurs almost year round, peaking in August and September. Although the turtles and their eggs are protected, there is no hatchery as on Pulau Selingan off Sandakan. Take your torch a member of Borneo Divers' staff, walk quietly along the shore and wait until you see a turtle – so fast and graceful underwater – out of her element lumbering awkwardly up the beach, to dig a hole with her flippers before laying her eggs. Do not use a camera flash before the turtle starts laying, or she may take fright and return to the sea.

Sipadan Island is, quite simply, an untouched jewel both above and below the water. Discover it before the rest of the world does.

In the Virgin Rainforest

Experience the most complex ecosystem on earth in the rainforest of Danum Valley, where you may encounter honking hornbills, elephants, all 10 species of Sabah's primates, bears, wild cats, deer and rare birds such as the Argus Pheasant.

Before visiting Danum Valley Conservation Area, make reservations (see "Where to Stay"), book your flight to Lahad Datu on Sabah's east coast and read Trekking & Wildlife Observation ("See Travel Essentials"). If you arrive on a Monday, Wednesday or Friday, you'll be met at Lahad Datu airport by transport for Yayasan Sabah, in whose vast 100-year logging concession Danum Valley is located. (Yayasan Sabah's transport service costs M$30; otherwise hire a mini-bus for M$130 one way.)

Opened in 1986 as a centre for conservation, research and educa-tion, the 438-square-kilometre Danum Valley Conservation Area offers visitors the rare opportunity to observe the virgin lowland rainforest where scientists are carrying out research, and where young Sabahans are being taught to know and care for their unique environment.

You will probably have time for lunch and a quick look at the old shops built over the bay at the end of Lahad Datu's main street before leaving for Danum Valley. For good Chinese-style seafood, try Kedai Makan Seng Kee, in the lane just beyond the Standard Chartered Bank. The 1½-hour trip to Danum Valley takes you near Mount Silam, with glimpses of beautiful Darvel Bay to your left, before turning inland.

An international-standard lodge is planned for Danum Valley, but in the meantime, you stay at the Field Centre in either the comfortable hostel or resthouse near the Segama River. On arrival, go to the Reception Centre to familiarise yourself with the layout of the Field Centre and the trails, pur-chase leech socks and brochures for self-guided nature walks, and arrange for your first walk in the forest with a junior guide. (This is compulsory to minimise risk of visitors getting lost or inadver-tently interfering with on-going research projects.) To obtain the maximum from your visit, hire a specialised guide with scientific training for at least one trail walk, when the magic of the rain-forest will be revealed as never before.

On your first morning, get up at day break and watch the forest awakening. Cross the suspension bridge – probably still swathed in mist – and walk along one of the western trails. Amidst a cons-tant chorus of birdsong, you may hear the calls of the gibbons, see

Prolific fungi

an orang-utan leaving the nest where he's spent the night, catch sight of a tiny mouse-deer, or see the rich auburn Red Leaf Monkeys out looking for breakfast. In the cool of the early morning, the forest positively seethes with life.

The heat builds up by mid-day, when only the shrilling cicadas, the odd darting lizard and clouds of brilliant butterflies seem to be moving. If the water level is not too high, walk up the Segama River in old clothes and a pair of trainers, watching for the clouds of butterflies feeding from the pools or on patches of urine left by animals on the sand. You may catch sight of an otter or mongoose, or even be lucky enough to see elephants coming down to drink. For a unique river ride, launch yourself into the water and drift back down to the Field Centre.

The afternoon is a good time for the shaded riverine trail. For additional excitement, arrange for a guide to take you across to the burial caves. It was the custom for the original inhabitants of this region, the Orang Sungei (literally "River People") to bury their dead in caves. After crossing the Segama, you scrabble up the hillside, feeling a bit like Indiana Jones as you push aside lianas and crouch under a limestone overhang to view old Chinese ceramic burial jars and carved wooden coffins discovered only in 1990, and thought to be about three centuries old.

Late afternoon is one of the best times for bird watching. The tower located just off the approach road to the Centre gives you a comfortable seat high above the forest; armed with a pair of binoculars, you can be sure of spotting several species of hornbill and a good number of the other 240 species of birds recorded at Danum Valley to date.

Around 6.15 to 6.30 pm, be sure to sit on the suspension bridge to watch the Giant Flying Squirrels come out of their holes on a nearby tree to leap across the river, gliding for as much as 300 metres thanks to the membrane between their front and back limbs. The next thrill of the evening will be the Buffy Fish Owl which comes near the badminton court to wait for the insects and moths attracted by the bright lights.

For the ultimate in evening

Fruit bat

entertainment, go on a night drive. Standing in the back of a moving jeep, you swing a spotlight until it reflects from the mirror of some nocturnal creature's eyes. More lights are flashed and a striped civet cat is revealed, or maybe an owl, a squirrel or a tarsier, a bizarre little creature which obviously inspired the creators of the movie "E.T".

You may not see a rare rhino, a sun bear, an elephant or any other the other large mammals known to inhabit Danum Valley, but the untouched beauty of the rainforest, its birds and insects, its profusion of plants and the way in which the entire ecosystem is so brilliantly orchestrated is something you'll never forget.

Down Among the Muruts

Scale the sheer limestone pinnacle of Batu Punggul after travelling upriver in one of the most remote regions of Sabah, not far from the Kalimantan border. You'll enjoy the rice wine and hospitality of the Murut tribe, many of whom still follow their traditional ways.

The purpose of this trip is as much to travel as to arrive, with the actual scaling of Batu Punggul merely an excuse to explore part of the heartland of Borneo. Unless you have plenty of time and, preferably, speak some Malay, you'll find it much easier to get to Batu Punggul through a tour operator. Otherwise, travel by minibus to Sapulut (via Keningau) and arrange for the next stage of your trip through Lantir or another member of the Bakayas family, who run Sapulut Adventures. It's a good idea to buy some fruit,

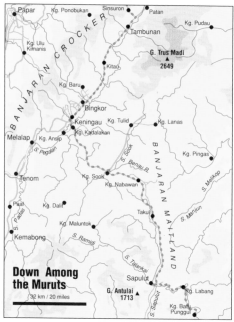

biscuits and other snacks to supplement your diet before leaving KK; don't forget to pack insect repellent, some warm clothing, gloves, sunhat and shoes or trainers suitable for scaling the limestone outcrop of Batu Punggul.

The round trip takes a minimum of three days, sometimes four. It begins with a long drive to Sapulut, across the Crocker Range

Murut dancers

and down through the village of Tambunan to Keningau, a bustling, unlovely centre for the 40 sawmills in the district. From here, you really start travelling as the unsealed road takes you southeast through an often devastated landscape, with dozens of logging trucks hauling giants of the forest or tonnes of sawn timber, turning the road to either a blinding cloud of dust or a quagmire, depending on the season.

About half way between Keningau and Sapulut, Kampung Nabawan comes as something of a surprise: a neat little town with about 3 kilometres of sealed road and even street signs. In the early 1970s, the government felt that Pensiangan was too inaccessible and transferred its district headquarters to the newly created township of Nabawan. However, the Muruts were reluctant to exchange their rich hunting and fishing area for the poor soil and limited possibilities of Nabawan, which remains under-populated to this day.

After Nabawan, the road becomes interesting, with patches of undisturbed forest, glimpses of river and remarkable wooden Murut graves, built like miniature houses, at the roadside. Stop and look at the carving and painting or, on more modern graves, gay bunting looking like a medieval knight's banner. You may even spot one very old grave where a pottery urn containing the remains of the departed stands under a roof.

Just before Sapulut, you cross your first log bridge. Massive tree trunks are laid in 6 or 7 layers, each at right angles to the previous layer, to form a support for the trunks that extend across the river. Seemingly indestructible, these bridges have a lifespan of only five years or so, since they're used by logging trucks carrying an enormous weight of felled trees.

Sapulut is less a village than a scattering of simple houses, a health clinic and a school, on either side of the river. A couple of rudimentary stores (one operated by the Bakayas family) cater to the villagers, as does the river (with a supply of fish that are netted several times a day) and the forest (where deer and pig are sometimes hunted). Famed for his skill with a blowpipe, today's Murut hunter is more likely to go out with a gun, but still with his faithful dog trotting along behind.

(You may be interested to know that it is possible – if you have an Indonesian visa, plenty of time and money – to travel downriver from Sapulut to the Pensiangan River, crossing into Kalimantan and following the Sembakung River all the way to the east coast, near Tarakan.)

If the drive from KK has been fast (6 or 7 hours) and if the boat-man in Sapulut is fully organised, it will be possible to go directly on to the Batu Punggul area, arriving around night-fall. Otherwise, you'll stay in Sapulut, where your accommodation is a bark-walled hut with a long verandah and "kitchen" where a flying fox skin may be drying beside the open hearth, and with the river doing duty as the "bathroom". Be pre-pared for a cool evening, as the altitude of around 300 metres to-gether with the nearby river and lush vegetation of the interior makes a chilly contrast to coas-tal temperatures.

Dainty deer

You'll travel by long wooden canoe with an out-board engine upriver to Kampung Tatalan, and then on another 10 minutes or so to where simple accommodation was opened at the end of 1991. The journey upriver, like so many other trips in Borneo, depends entirely on conditions. If the river level is low, you'll need to help haul the boat over the shallow rapids; if it's very high, the current will slow you down. Be prepared for 4-7 hours travel, passing several longhouse settlements en route.

About three-quarters of the way to Kampung Tatalan, you get the chance to stretch your legs at a point where the river does a giant loop. The boatman prefers to have a lighter load for negotiating the rapids along this part of the river, so you walk across a narrow neck of land at Kampung Labang, meeting the boat about half an hour later.

Kampung Tatalan consists of a longhouse of about 7-10 families, and is the last settlement before the new Batu Punggol Resort, on the river bank near the base of Batu Punggul. (If you prefer to stay in the genuine longhouse at Kampung Tatalan, you can request this in advance.) The climb to the limestone outcrop begins in the cooler hours of early morning, and involves a walk of about 20 minutes along a steep, often slippery track through primary rainforest. The sheer pinnacle of Batu Punggul looks unscalable from some angles, but you'll approach from around the back, along a ridge that avoids a yawning chasm of 80-100 metres. You'll have time to explore a small cave, one of many in the outcrop, then it's onward and upward for almost an hour.

Experts swear that Batu Punggul is not difficult to climb, and ropes are not necessary, but you certainly need a good head for heights. At times, you feel like a fly climbing a wall, but it's all worth while as you stand on top, gazing back down river towards Tatalan. If you've still got the energy after your climb, ask your guide to show you the huge network of caves about 15 minutes from the main track. A cathedral could fit inside one of the caves, where swifts' nests are gathered in season.

Your day will probably be capped by an evening's entertainment with the Muruts of Kampung Tatalan, when you'll be able to sample the famous *tapai* (rice wine) sipped from a pottery jar through a reed. In days gone by, traditional dances would be performed spontaneously for guests, but the practice of paying for dances to be performed for tourists has been introduced by some of the tour companies. This does not, however, diminish the very real welcome you will be given by the local Muruts, and the dances and costumes remain impressive. It's all a very long way – both literally and figuratively – from downtown Kota Kinabalu, but a journey well worth making.

Giant dipterocarp tree, Murut elder (right)

Nightlife

To most people in Sabah, nightlife means sitting around over a good meal and maybe a drink or two with family or friends – if you're looking for wild, raunchy times, you've come to the wrong place. This is not to say you can't have fun, especially in Kota Kinabalu and other big towns.

The most popular form of entertainment currently is karaoke, where anyone visiting the karaoke lounge can just pick up the mike and become an instant star, singing along to a recorded orchestra while following words on a video screen. Needless to say, the quality varies enormously but everyone seems to have a lot of fun. There are also discos and music lounges, many with karaoke lounge attached.

In Kota Kinabalu, it is possible to see a cultural show (Malam Kampung) at the Tanjung Aru Resort at 8 pm every Sunday, with local songs, dances and costumes featured in the Garden Restaurant. Popular, so book if you want to dine on the Malaysian buffet while watching the show.

Some other places where you might like to check out the nightlife include:

Sedco Square
Kampung Air
Kota Kinabalu
An open-air square where tables and food stalls are set up each night; several restaurants around the square do a good business in seafood, satay, noodle dishes etc., while a lot of the local lads like to sit around over a beer watching the world go by. Nothing fancy, but pleasant on a warm tropical night; prices are reasonable, and you can see how some Sabahans enjoy their evenings.

Disco dancing

Jaws Karaoke Lounge
4th fl Gaya Centre
Jalan Tun Fuad Stephens
Tel: 236008
Located inside a big Thai-Chinese restaurant, this karaoke lounge
is popular with both locals and visitors.

Tiffiny Discotheatre
Block A No.9, Jalan Karamunsing
Tel: 218091/210645
Disco with karaoke lounge popular with the younger set.

Heartbeat
No 22, Karamunsing Warehouse
Jalan Sembulan Lama
Tel: 225880
A three-in-one entertainment complex with disco, Nostalgia Lounge
bar with songs to take you down memory lane, and a karaoke lounge
for would-be singers. One of KK's most popular night spots.

Chinese fan dance

EATING OUT

Sabah's magnificent seafood — succulent scallops, giant prawns, lobsters, moon-white squid, glistening fresh fish and meaty crabs — is joined by a cornucopia of tropical fruits and vegetables, as well as cool-climate produce from the mountainsides. These superb natural ingredients combined with the culinary expertise of Sabah's many different ethnic groups promise the visitor an almost endless variety of dining experiences, and at remarkably reasonable prices too.

The indigenous cuisines range from the fish-oriented diet of the coastal Bajao, Suluk and Idahan to the jungle produce — wild pig, deer, river fish, ferns and other wild vegetables — of the interior folk such as the Kadazan and Murut. It is not easy to find traditional Sabahan food in the restaurants and food stalls, for these are dominated by Chinese, Malay, Indian and Indonesian chefs, many of them relatively recent arrivals whose food has been enthusiastically adopted by the original Sabahans.

Those with a liking for other Asian cuisines will also find Japanese, Thai and Korean restaurants, while lovers of Western food can indulge in French, Italian and English dishes as well as American "fast food" in Kota Kinabalu and some other major towns.

Popular Local Dishes

Some of the dishes you are likely to encounter in local restaurants, coffee shops and food stalls include:

Banana Leaf Curry: no, you don't eat the leaves, but the tasty Southern Indian vegetable, fish, chicken or meat curries that are served on a square of freshly-cut banana leaf. You can usually order *dosai*, wafer-thin rice and lentil flour pancakes eaten with savoury dips, at such establishments.

Barbecued Seafood: don't miss this treat of ray, fish, squid or prawns, bathed with a spicy sauce, wrapped in banana leaf and grilled over charcoal.

Chicken Rice: Hainanese favourite which is simple but delicious; tender chicken served with rice, cucumber, soup and a savoury chilli-ginger side dish (*sambal*).

Coto: (pronounced "choto")

Makassar: a robust Indonesian beef soup with chunks of rice cake, spiced with chilli.

Fresh produce for the kitchen

Dim Sum: steamed or deep fried titbits usually served at breakfast; stuffed white buns with roasted pork (*char siew pow*) or redbean paste (*tau sa pow*), tiny dumplings filled with pork (*siew mai*) and pork ribs steamed with black beans (*pai kwat*) are most commonly found in coffee shops. Look for stacks of big round woven bamboo steaming baskets.

Kway Teow: wide fresh rice-flour noodles prepared either fried (*goreng*) or in a soup.

Laksa: a spicy Malay soup, usually enriched with coconut milk and chock full of prawns, chicken, noodles and beansprouts.

Mee: wheat-flour noodles served in a variety of ways, often fried with pork, prawns and vegetables or served in a soup.

Meehoon (also beehoon): dried rice-flour vermicelli, prepared wet or dry as for mee.

Nasi Campur: pronounced "*champur*", this is steamed rice with several savoury Malay vegetable, chicken, seafood or beef dishes which the diner chooses himself from the cooked food on display. Always good value.

Nasi Goreng: fried rice.

Nasi Padang: West Sumatran style of cooking, often toned down in Sabah but normally redolent with spices and chillies; the coconut beef (*rendang*), curried brains (*otak*) and mild sweet coconut-milk chicken (*opor ayam*) are some of the most popular dishes eaten with rice.

Kadazan speciality "hinava"

Ngau chap: Chinese noodle soup full of various portions of beef.

Roti Canai: light, flaky Indian bread fried on a griddle and served with lentils (*dhal*) or curry gravy. Excellent for breakfast or as a snack.

Satay: Malaysian favourite of seasoned skewered beef, chicken or mutton grilled over charcoal and served with spicy peanut sauce.

Soto: Malay/Javanese soup made with spices, chicken, beansprouts, potato and sometimes chunks of steamed rice cake. Added heat provided by a side dish of chilli *sambal*.

Tom Yam Noodles: based on the favourite Thai soup redolent with lemon, chillies and prawns, the local version adds lots of coconut milk and oil, as well as the noodles of your choice.

Some Popular Drinks

The usual canned and packaged drinks, including (unless it is a Muslim establishment) beer and stout, are available in coffee shops and restaurants throughout Sabah. Wine is available only at a very few Western restaurants and the major hotels. Some other drinks you might like to try here include:

Cendol: somewhere between a dessert and a drink, this is a combination of coconut milk, palm sugar syrup and jelly-like bright green strips made from mung pea flour.

Fresh fruit juice: some food stalls, especially in modern shopping complexes, offer freshly made juices; try sweet avocado shake, starfruit, papaya with banana or watermelon with orange. Tell the vendor if you do not want added sugar.

Leong foon: squares of black jelly made from a type of seaweed combined with coconut milk and sugar syrup; believed to be cooling by the Chinese.

Limau kasturi: the juice of fresh small fragrant limes, often served with a few sour dried Chinese plums (*ham moy*).

Sabah's unique red-fleshed durian

While you're here, don't miss the chance to sample a couple of unique vegetables. *Sayur manis* (also known as Sabah *choy*, Sabah vegetable or Sabah asparagus) is a local vegetable that has been developed to produce slender, crunchy stems with tender leaves at the top. Stir fried with *sambal belacan* (a spicy paste) or dried prawns, or simply bathed with oyster sauce, the vegetable has a texture vaguely reminiscent of just-cooked asparagus but a flavour all its own. Take a leaf out of the jungle dweller's book and try young fern tips (*pakis*), cooked in similar ways to the *sayur manis*; very good to eat and full of minerals too. Although *shiitake* mushrooms are not indigenous, they grow well on the slopes of the Crocker Range close to Kota Kinabalu; often called Sabah mushrooms and served in most Chinese restaurants, they are excellent braised with oyster sauce.

Soya bean milk *(susu kachang)*: sweetened soya bean milk.

Tapai: the local rice wine, not normally available in coffee shops but found in local markets (*tamu*) and at any Kadazan or Murut festival. Somewhat like Japanese sake. The best, Lihing No. 1, is made in Tambunan.

Young green coconut: enjoy the refreshing, pure liquid from a young coconut, usually available at beachside stalls.

Local Fruits

Apart from offering the usual tempting range of tropical fruits such as mango, papaya, pineapple and banana, Sabah has a great many unique fruits which have marketing potential. On one occasion, arranged for a group of fruit enthusiasts from overseas, a total of 43 wild fruits was served! Some 15 or so varieties of mango are found, as well as a red-fleshed durian and other strange delights.

In the markets, fruit you are likely to come across (apart from the usual bananas, mangoes, papaya and pineapple) include:

Chiku: the South American sapodilla, this is a pale brown egg-shaped fruit that should be eaten when just starting to soften; it tastes like pears flavoured with maple syrup.

Durian: notorious for its pungent smell, this strange fruit looks like a spiky football. Inside are segments of buttery flesh which taste either like heaven or hell, depending on your personal reaction. Worth trying at least once. (Look for durians just outside the entrance to Poring Hot Springs in the Kinabalu National Park; the tree there provides some superb fruit during the season, usually August/September. The unique red durians can be found in Season Beaufort market.)

Langsat: also known by their Filipino name, lanzones, they're small

Array of local fruit

beige fruits enclosing segments of very sweet, juicy white flesh around non-edible seeds.

Mangosteen: purplish black skin (that stains permanently) with remarkably flavoured sweet-sour juicy segments with a non-edible seed.

Pomelo: giant yellow citrus fruit with very thick skin; either yellow or pink-fleshed inside, often very sweet and juicy.

Rambutan: hairy red exterior, sweet white flesh and non-edible seed.

Starfruit: yellow with five-ridges, rather like a torpedo; sweet yet faintly astringent, juicy and very refreshing.

Where to Eat

The ubiquitous *kedai kopi* or coffee shop is a Malaysian institution found all over Sabah, offering not only hot and cold drinks but food, often prepared by stall holders who sublet from the owner. Food here is often very good and inexpensive. Don't ignore the rickety foodstalls either; you can often tell by the BMWs and expensive 4-wheel drives that even the wealthiest gourmets don't turn their noses up at the surroundings if the food is good.

Many restaurants are simple, open-fronted shophouses, cooled by ceiling fans and usually very moderately priced. They rarely have menus and diners simply look at all the basic ingredients in the kitchen and make their requests accordingly. The cook or owner is invariably happy to make suggestions. Airconditioned restaurants serving Chinese, Malay, Indian and other Asian cuisines, or various Western cuisines are found in the towns and in major hotels.

Local stallfood served in comfortable surroundings and Western fastfood such as fried chicken and pizzas can be found in large air-conditioned shopping complexes such as Centrepoint.

Eating places outside of Kota Kinabalu are recommended in the various itineraries. Some places you might like to try while in Kota Kinabalu include:

Kadazan

Yun Chuan Kedai Kopi & Makan

Block l, Lot 8, Penampang New
Town
Tel: 712004

One of the few places to try authentic Kadazan food is this open-fronted restaurant overlooking an open green at the back of a group of new shophouses about 8 km from Kota Kinabalu. Dishes such as *hinava* (raw fish marinated in lime and mixed with ginger, garlic, chilli, onions and celery leaf), chicken and rice wine (*tapai*) soup and *pakis* (fern tips) cooked with *sambal* are normally available at lunch time. To be sure of Kadazan specialities, phone Chong Pak Leong in advance; he will arrange a complete Kadazan meal if requested.

Seafood

Chuan Hin

Jalan Kolam (next to Cottage Pub),
Luyang
Tel: 235960

Very good, inexpensive barbecued seafood (especially ray and squid), *woh teh* dumplings and fried *kway teow* noodles. Casual open-fronted establishment about 10 minutes from downtown KK. Barbecued food served from 6 pm to midnight.

Port View Seafood Restaurant

Jalan Haji Saman (opposite the Marine Police)
Tel: 221753

Open only in the evenings from 6 am through to 2 am, this is a very popular, unpretentious restaurant serving live seafood. Their *assam pedas* (fish curry) and steamed fish are both recommended. *Satay* on sale at a stall just outside.

100% Seafood Restaurant

Jalan Aru, Tanjung Aru Beach
Tel: 238313

Market-style display of fresh fish and seafood which you select and have cooked whatever way you want. Good garlic rice and fresh vegetables to go with your seafood. Wine and beer also available.

Wind Bell Seafood Restaurant

20 Jalan Selangor, Tanjung Aru
Beach
Tel: 222305

Open for both lunch and dinner, they specialise in live seafood and steamboat, a type of fondue in which an array of fish, meat and vegetables are cooked at the table by diners. Moderately priced. Free transportation service back to hotel for visitors at night.

Chinese

Nan Xing Hotel & Restaurant

Jalan Pantai
Tel: 212900/212399

Popular for *dim sum* in the mornings (especially Sunday) and for traditional Cantonese cuisine in cool comfortable surroundings. Located in downtown KK.

Sam Sui Kedai Kopi

Putatan

Situated in a new block of shophouses just to the right of the main road as you enter the village of Putatan, about 7 km from Kota Kinabalu, this coffee shop sells a variety of Chinese food but draws people from all over town at lunch time for the best *tom yam* noodles around.

Sembulan Foodstalls

off Jalan Sembulan

Open only in the evenings, makeshift tables and chairs are set up outside three simple kitchens producing whatever you fancy from an assortment of ingredients. Turn into Jalan Sembulan off the Coastal Highway, then take the second road to the left. Just a few metres from the corner, and on the right, are the kitchens; the one on the far left is best. Recommended dishes include chicken and rice wine (*tapai*) soup, sweet and sour fish and *sayur manis* vegetable. Very cheap.

East and West

Wishbone Cafe

Hotel Jesselton, 69 Gaya Street
Tel: 55633

Pleasant, comfortable airconditioned cafe popular at lunchtime for its varied menu of favourite Chinese and Malay dishes (the Hainanese Chicken Rice is good) plus a few Western items. Near the banks and Sabah Tourism Promotion Council. Slightly pricier than the coffee shops, but worth it for the comfort.

Malay
Sri Rahmat
Lorong Tiong Hwa (2nd pedestrian mall), Segama Complex
Right in the centre of Segama complex in downtown KK, this is a good place for lunch, having an airconditioned dining section. *Nasi campur*, where you choose ready cooked dishes to accompany your rice, is good here. Open until 9pm.

Sri Sempeleng
Jalan Sembulan
Not far from the mosque, fire station and government offices, this open-fronted eating house attracts enthusiastic diners for its Malay and Indonesian food. Their *soto ayam*, a noodle soup made with free-range *kampung* chickens, is popular.

Restoran Kampung Air
#9, Block F, Sadong Jaya (behind Komplex Kuasa, Karamunsing
Tel: 238849
An array of good ready cooked Malay food from which you can serve yourself, smorgasbord style, as well as noodles, Western dishes and locally raised rabbit cooked both Asian and Western style. Semi-open air, decorated with basketware, bamboo and potted plants, with an airconditioned dining room. Unusual for a restaurant serving Malay food, beer is available. Open 24 hours a day.

Indian
Sri Madras Banana Leaf Curry House
Bandaran Berjaya
(in block next to Hotel Shangrila; Premas Letrik on corner)
A little out of the way but worth hunting for, this has the best *dosai* (crispy pancakes) in town; specialises

in southern Indian cuisine served on a banana leaf. Vegetarian meals available. Inexpensive but no beer served.

Restoran Bilal
Ruang Antarabangsa (first pedestrian mall)
Segama Complex
Good flaky Indian bread (*roti canai*) and richly flavoured curries to go with them; chicken liver is particularly good. Casual open-fronted restaurant right in centre of KK. Open until 8pm.

Thai
Jaws Restaurant
4th fl, Gaya Centre, Jalan Haji Saman
Tel: 236006/236008
Fine Thai-Chinese cuisine beautifully presented in elegant surroundings. Expensive but good.

Korean
Korea House
Block closest to Padang in Bandaran Berjaya
Tel: 58127/237401
Airconditioned restaurant serving Korean favourites at modest prices. Illustrated menu makes selection easier for those unfamiliar with this robust, often spicy cuisine.

Japanese
Azuma
Wisma Merdeka, Jalan Tun Razak
Tel: 2225533
The best Japanese food in town served in traditional surroundings with the usual *sushi* bar and a menu of popular Japanese dishes. Authentic food at the higher prices one always expects to pay for Japanese cuisine.

Western Food
Pepino's
Tanjung Aru Resort, Tanjung Aru
Tel: 58711/225800
Attractive but unpretentious restaurant with popular Italian dishes and wine. One of the best dishes is ravioli stuffed with gorgonzola cheese. Very good service but expensive.

Fish drying in the tropical sun

Shopping

The best place for souvenirs, handicrafts and gift items is Kota Kinabalu and the Kinabalu National Park, except for the odd item you may spot at a local *tamu* (weekly market). You will find not only typically Sabahan goods but a wide range of popular items from Peninsular Malaysia. In Kota Kinabalu's Filipino market, there is also a selection of inexpensive handicrafts and clothing from the Philippines, plus a few items from Sarawak and Indonesia. It is difficult to find antique items, although these may on occasion appear in gift shops such as the Sabah Handicraft Centre.

Sabahan Products

Basketware: a wide range of items, ranging from the gaily coloured conical Badjao food covers to the typical Kadazan carrying basket, from the finely woven Rungus reedwork to Murut and Kadazan hats. One of Sabah's best buys.

Batik: although this is not a traditional local art form, a couple of artists are producing lovely paintings, pareos, parasols and other items with local motifs, including orchids, coral reefs, fish and typical scenery.

Kadazan woven backpacks (wakid)

Beads: occasionally, valuable antique beads can be purchased, but most commonly, you will find brightly coloured necklaces, belts and other items made by Rungus women from tiny modern beads of plastic.

Dastar: intricately woven cloth squares, usually with geometric designs, these are folded and worn as headdresses by Kadazan, Rungus, Illanun and Bajao men. They look good framed, or can be used as a cushion cover.

Insects/Specimens: dramatic rhinoceros beetles, scorpions, brilliantly disguised stick insects, butterflies pressed onto a book mark and other specimens of insects make an unusual gift. Environmental concerns preclude the commercial processing of such items in Sabah, although insects and butterflies from Peninsular Malaysia can be found here.

Semporna pearls

Mats: Handwoven mats made from pandanus leaf and other soft grasses are a speciality of the Bajaos, although several other ethnic groups also produce them. Colourful and washable.

Pearls: Pearls cultivated off Semporna on the east coast of Sabah can be bought either loose or set in many jewellery and gift shops; either round or large, flat pearls can be found in cream, pink and grey-black tones and are reasonably priced.

Pottery: There are several potteries on the outskirts of Kota Kinabalu, producing domestic items as well as ornamental pieces. Many are incised with traditional motifs, while a couple of potters are also making attractive unglazed jars and vases in classical Chinese shapes.

Sabah Mushrooms: If you live within just a few hours' flying time of Kota Kinabalu, you might consider taking back a bag of the succulent, fresh brown mushrooms usually known by their Japanese name (*shiitake*) and found dried in Asian food stores around the world. Buy them from the Central Market or at the speciality mushroom shop at Kota Kinabalu Airport. Usually about M$10 per 500g.

Shells: A reminder of Sabah's beautiful waters, local shells can be found in one KK shop specialising in these. A wide range of shells from the Philippines (many of them identical to those found in Sabah) are sold in the Filipino market.

Spices: Attractively packed sets of local spices, including cinnamon, pepper and cloves, can be found in some gift shops.

Souvenirs from Sabah waters

Sompoton: This Kadazan instrument is made from several bamboo tubes with a dried gourd at the base. Light to carry and distinctively Sabahan.

Weaving: The Rungus women have long been renowned for their cloth woven on a backstrap loom. Full length skirts are seldom made today, but it is possible to find smaller cloth rectangles (dastars) as well as strips that can be worn as belts or incorporated in cushion covers or clothes.

Other Malaysian Items

Batik: lengths of batik fabric as well as ready made clothing, scarfs, hangings, hats and so on are sold in all the gift shops. Attractively packaged silk scarves make an excellent gift.

Pewter: Good quality pewter made from Malaysia's abundant supplies of tin is sold in a wide variety of designs.

Where to Buy

Wisma Merdeka, Wisma Sabah and Centrepoint offer a wide range of shops including a major Japanese department store. Bargaining is not the normal practice in stores where prices are marked, although if you buy a number of items you might be able to have the overall price reduced. For gift items and souvenirs, try:

Borneo Gifts
G 22, Wisma Sabah
Jalan Haji Saman
One of the biggest selections of quality gift items from both

Sabah and Peninsular Malaysia, including batik clothing, tee-shirts, pewter, maps, greeting cards etc.

Borneo Handicraft
Lot A148, 1st fl, Wisma Merdeka
Jalan Tun Razak
Wide selection of local handicrafts and souvenirs, including the best range of pottery to be found anywhere. They have another shop on the ground floor of Centrepoint, Classic Batik & Craft.

Borneo Craft
BG 26, Ground fl. Wisma Merdeka, Phasa II
Jalan Tun Razak
A well chosen selection of local and other Malaysian items, as well as the best selection of books on the region available in Kota Kinabalu.

Filipino Market
Jalan Tun Fuad Stephens
A rabbit-warren of stalls selling handbags, baskets, carvings, jewellery, shells, embroidered clothing and a host of handicrafts from the Philippines, as well as a selection of Indonesian batik and some basketware from Sarawak. Be sure to bargain.

Kinabalu Souvenirs
Kinabalu National Park Headquarters
This souvenir shop has some interesting gifts not found elsewhere, such as a cassette tape of the bird songs of Mount Kinabalu, book marks set with butterflies and wildflowers and books on Borneo as well as the usual tee-shirts, postcards etc.

Sabah Handicrafts
Lot 49, Bandaran Berjaya
(next to Hotel Shangrila)
This shop specialises in Sabahan handicrafts, including an irresistibly cuddly stuffed toy orang-utan. They also sell a few items from Sarawak and a small selection of books. Occasional antique items. Slightly out of the way but worth the detour.

Sports

With its superb beaches and clear waters, mountains, forests and rivers, Sabah offers the sports lover plenty of opportunities. You can tee off at a golf course carved from the forest almost 2,000 metres up a mountain, scuba dive around one of the world's most remarkable oceanic islands, shoot the rapids in a raging river, horse ride along a beach, fish for barracuda, speed over the waves in a Hobie cat or play tennis in the cool hours of dusk.

Scuba Diving

Clear, unpolluted waters, coral reefs and literally dozens of islands – including Pulau Sipadan, Malaysia's only oceanic island rising up 600 metres from the ocean floor – make Sabah ideal for scuba diving. It is possible to explore the reefs of islands just 20 minutes from Kota Kinabalu, or to go further afield. Resort courses introducing novices to the sport are available in Kota Kinabalu, while divers with proof of certification can do either individual day dives, night dives, or enjoy a diving package. Main diving operators in Sabah are:

Coral reefs bathed by translucent water

Diving opportunities abound

Borneo Divers & Sea Sports

4th fl, Wisma Sabah
Jalan Haji Saman
Kota Kinabalu
Locked Bag 194, 88999 Kota Kinabalu, Sabah, Malaysia
Tel: (088) 222226
Fax: (088) 221550

Sabah's biggest and most professional operator, offering diving around Kota Kinabalu as well as package dive holidays at their Sipadan Island Dive Lodge. Single dives in KK (including transport, tanks and belt) cost M$65, night dives M$100. The 5-day Padi Open Water Diver course costs from M$650-M$900, depending upon the number of divers. Diving packages at Pulau Sipadan, which include all transport, accommodation, food and unlimited diving cost from US$500 for 2 days/1 night to US$700 for 5 days/4 nights. Borneo Divers also has a shop selling all types of diving equipment on the ground floor of Wisma Sabah.

Borneo Sea Adventures

1st fl, 8A Karamunsing Warehouse
Kota Kinabalu
P.O. Box 10134, 88801 Kota Kinabalu, Sabah, Malaysia
Tel: (088) 55390/221106
Fax: (088) 221106

Specialises in diving and diver training around Kota Kinabalu, although they will organise diving holidays at Pulau Sipadan. Their charges for a single dive are M$60, night dive M$80, 3-day Open Water Diving Course M$650, 4-day Pulau Sipadan package including all transport, accommodation, food and unlimited diving M$1,344.

Coral Island Cruises
G 19, ground fl, Wisma Sabah
Jalan Haji Saman
Kota Kinabalu
P.O. Box 14527, 88851 Kota Kinabalu, Sabah, Malaysia
Tel: (088) 223490/239349
Fax: (088) 223404
Their comfortable 46-metre cruise ship, *Coral Topaz*, offers diving
as well as fishing holidays to the remote atoll of Layang Layang,
some 165 nautical miles northwest of Kota Kinabalu. They also
arrange weekend trips to Pulau Tiga, just 28 miles from KK, where
the flora and fauna of this protected island are as interesting as the
reefs surrounding it.

Kota Aquatics
AG04 Wisma Merdeka
Jalan Tun Razak
Kota Kinabalu
Tel/fax: (088) 218710
Diver training, plus sale of diving, fishing, sporting and camping
equipment. Owner Peter Chang is a marine biologist who also acts
as a field agent for foreign scientific expeditions in Sabah.

White-Water Rafting

Sabah's rivers range from great wide waterways snaking through
mangrove forest to clear mountains streams that join each other to
become fast-flowing rivers carving their way through gorges on their
headlong rush towards the South China Sea. Luckily for the visitor,
the best rivers for rafting are within easy reach of Kota Kinabalu,
and range from a gentle float through delightful rural scenery to
adrenalin-pumping fights around huge boulders and across tumul-
tuous rapids.

Several tour companies offer a package which includes a ride by
quaint railcar to the launching site on the Padas River, followed by
an often hair-raising ride back down river. The Padas is at its most
exciting after rain in the interior. Contact Api Tours, tel: (088)
221233 or Discovery Tours, tel: (088) 215584.

Other Water Sports

Despite their tremendous potential, water sports are not yet widely
available in Sabah, currently being limited to the Kota Kinabalu
area. There are two marinas located on the water's edge at Tanjung
Aru Resort ("The Marina" and Transworld), offering ferry services
to the nearby islands of the Tunku Abdul Rahman Park, as well as

Traditional way of river rafting

rental of equipment. Check out both marinas before making your decision, as the standard of gear varies. Hire costs are: snorkel equipment (M$20 per day); windsurfers (M$35 per hour), Hobie cat (M$40 per hour), water scooters (M$60 per hour); water skiing (M$120 per hour) para-sailing (M$80).

Sailing enthusiasts may be able to enjoy an hour or so as crew on one of the sailing dinghies in races organised by the Kinabalu Yacht Club, Tanjung Aru Beach. Ask at the Club around noon on a Saturday or Sunday.

Hobie cat nea

Fishing

The waters just off Kota Kinabalu are not as rich in big fish as those further afield, especially near places such as Pulau Mengalum, Mantanani and Layang Layang. Fishing trips, including night fishing, are available through Coral Island Cruises (see entry under Scuba Diving) as well as through The Marina, Tanjung Aru Beach Hotel, tel: 214215/232721/ 240955. Borneo Sea Adventures (see Scuba Diving) also arrange for game fishing.

Golf

With 7 golf courses around the state, visitors will find ample opportunity to indulge in a game. The premier club, Sabah Golf and Country Club, has an 18-hole course in Kota Kinabalu; telephone 224788 or 56533 to arrange a game. Don't forget to bring your handicap card with you. The Kinabalu Golf Club has a less challenging 9-hole course at Tanjung Aru Beach (tel: 51615).

Other courses are located at Sandakan, Ranau, Kudat and Keningau, with a particularly attractive and challenging course at 1,500 metres on the slopes of Mount Kinabalu. Arrange to hire clubs at Kinabalu Golf Club before heading off for this remote course on the slopes of the mountain, about ½ hour from the Kinabalu National Park Headquarters.

Golfing in KK

Hash House Harriers

A running fraternity founded in Malaysia, the "Hash", as it's affectionately known, organises runs three times a week in Kota Kinabalu. A good opportunity to explore the countryside and mix with local runners at drinks and dinner afterwards. Look in the "What's On" columns of the local daily newspapers.

Other Land Sports

The Likas Sports Complex in a suburb of Kota Kinabalu has excellent facilities for the following: swimming, tennis, squash and badminton, as well as offering a gymnasium.

Joggers will find the long, clean Tanjung Aru Beach ideal; go around 6 pm and take in the usually spectacular sunset as you finish your run.

Horse Riding

Gallop along the beach at sunrise, take a trail ride past the fields and *kampung* (villages) as you explore rural life, or ride at low tide across to a nearby island. Just 20 minutes by road from Kota Kinabalu is the small Kinarut Riding School, run by Dale Sinidol, (tel: 225525) who will collect you from your hotel and take you down to her beach-side stables for a ride. Prices from $50 for 1½ hours along the beach and islands, or $60 for the 2-hour *kampung* trail ride.

Calendar of Special Events

Thanks to its ethnic and religious diversity, Sabah celebrates a variety of traditional festivals, together with a number of unique sporting events. For the latest information on exact dates, contact the Sabah Tourism Promotion Council.

Chinese New Year (January/ February)

The start of the Lunar New Year is enthusiastically celebrated by Sabah's large Chinese community, with businesses and shops all over the state closing for their annual holiday. Prior to the New Year, goods spill out onto pavement stalls, tempting shoppers who indulge in an orgy of buying food, decorations, New Year cards, toys, flowers and fire crackers. The festival begins with a family reunion dinner on the eve of the New Year, which is ushered in by the blasting of fire crackers to scare away any evil spirits. The next couple of days are a round of feasting and visiting, with lion dances being performed outside many hotels and private homes. The lions continue to prowl, performing outside Chinese stores (which close for at least 2 days) with much clashing of cymbals, banging of drums and fire crackers on the last day of the 15-day New Year period (Chap Goh Mei).

Sabahans in traditional costume

Bajao horsement

Hari Raya Puasa

A Muslim festival to mark the end of Ramadan, the month in which Muslims are required to fast from sunrise to sunset. This begins with prayers of thanksgiving in mosques all over Sabah, followed by a round of feasting and visiting. Delicious cakes are a hallmark of the festival, and with typical generosity, Sabah's Muslims will often invite foreign visitors into their home to share the celebrations. Hari Raya is an excellent opportunity to photograph Muslims in traditional finery.

Pesta Ka'amatan/Harvest Festival (May)

Throughout the month of May, Kadazan/Dusun tribes celebrate the succesful harvesting of rice in villages all over the state, with ritual thanksgivings and a range of activities which culminate in the choosing of the Harvest Festival Queen (Unduk Ngadau). The festival is celebrated in Kota Kinabalu on 30th & 31st May at the Kadazan Dusun Cultural Association's headquarters, with cultural displays, traditional sports, handicraft demonstra-

tions and the choosing of the Harvest Queen. Harvest Festival dates in other locations can be obtained from the Sabah Tourism Promotion Council.

Sabah Fest (May)

Organised partly to give visitors an idea of the rich and diversified cultural heritage of Sabah, this includes a programme of cultural performances, cottage industries (weaving, basket making, beading and carving), a food fair and beach carnival. Lots of fun (and photographic opportunities) for all.

Vesak Day (May)

Buddhists celebrate the birth of Buddha with special prayers at temples, including a ritual washing of a statue of Buddha. The Goddess of Mercy (Kuan Yin) temple on Tuaran Road just before Inanam in Kota Kinabalu, and the big

Pui Gin Tsen Buddhist temple on a hilltop on the outskirts of Sandakan, are good places to go on the morning of Vesak Day.

Dragon Boat Festival (June)

A Chinese festival honouring a long-dead patriot, this is an exciting round of racing with international and local dragon boats – long wooden canoes manned by a crew of around 20 – fighting it out in the waters of Likas Bay near Kota Kinabalu town.

Birthday of the Yang di-Pertuan Agong (5th June)

A national festival honouring the supreme ruler (king) of Malaysia, celebrated with parades on KK's Padang (green colourful).

National Day (31st August)

Celebration of Malaysia's independence with parades and dancing.

Mount Kinabalu Climathon (September)

Held at Kinabalu Park, where climbers from many countries race to the summit and return. Normally a 10-hour trip for lesser mortals (who break their climb on the first day to sleep overnight on the mountain), the 1990 winner did it in an amazing 2 hours, 47 minutes.

Borneo Safari (October)

Starting in Kota Kinabalu, this rally is an opportunity for 4-wheel drive vehicles, including international participants, to discover the natural beauty and often-challenging conditions of driving in North Borneo.

Tamu

Once an occasion for often mutually hostile tribes to meet and barter their goods in peace, the weekly markets or *tamu* are still a popular institution in Sabah. Traders and buyers come from far and wide to buy medicine from a travelling salesman who exhibits crocodile heads as part of his act, to sell a buffalo, buy betel nut, catch up on gossip, buy some smoked wild pig and maybe down a convivial glass of rice wine (*tapai*). Although most tour operators take

Dragon Boat races

Kota Belud Sunday market

visitors to the Sunday morning markets at Kota Belud or Tuaran, others *tamus* are equally interesting, such as the Thursday market at Tambunan and Sikuati's market in Rungus territory near Kudat. The *tamu* offers the chance to pick up handicrafts, try local fruit and snacks and absorb the atmosphere. Some of the *tamus* you might find worth visiting if in the region include:

Beaufort	Saturday
Keningau	Thursday
Kinarut	Saturday
Kiulu	Tuesday
Kota Belud	Sunday
Kota Marudu	Sunday
Membakut	Sunday
Sikuati	Sunday
Sindumin	Saturday
Tambunan	Thurs/Sun
Tamparuli	Wednesday
Tenom	Sunday
Tuaran	Sunday

Gaya Street Fair

Kota Kinabalu's citified version of the *tamu*, when the end of Gaya Street is turned into an open-air market. From about 7 am until noon each Sunday, you can find everything from an orchid to a live rabbit, handicrafts to seasonal fruits, toys to the occasional antique. Go early for the best items and to avoid the heat.

Sabah Society Talks

The Sabah Society, an organisation devoted to furthering the knowledge of Sabah's history, culture and environment, holds talks in the theatre of the Sabah Museum in Kota Kinabalu, as well as outings to places of interest. Talks can be as diverse as a discussion of Death and Kinship Customs to the latest Borneo Safari Rally or the proboscis monkey. Look in the "What's On" column of the newspaper, or telephone 422211.

Tambunan tamu

Practical Information

When to Visit

Sabah enjoys a tropical climate, with temperatures ranging between about 22°C to 30°C in lowland areas throughout the year. Although rain can occur at any time of year, showers are generally brief. During the northwest monsoon (November to April), strong winds and heavy rain can occur, especially December through February on the east coast. The southwest monsoon, particularly during the months of July to September, brings rain to the west coast. Although there is no well defined visiting season, the best months to visit are between March and May; March is the most reliable month for climbing Mount Kinabalu, while May, when the whole state celebrates the Harvest Festival, is particularly colourful. July and August are normally very busy months, making it strongly advisable to book a hotel in Kota Kinabalu and accommodation at Kinabalu Park well in advance.

Getting There

Kota Kinabalu is connected by air with a number of regional capitals. The national carrier, MAS, operates daily flights from Kuala Lumpur, with other flights from Johore Baru, Singapore, Hong Kong, Taipei, Tokyo, Manila and Seoul. Flights from Sarawak and Labuan are also available, as well as a weekly flight connecting Tawau (on the east coast of Sabah) with Tarakan in Kalimantan, Indonesia. Cathay Pacific flies in from Hong Kong, while Singapore Airlines has two weekly flights from Singapore. Thai Airways connects Bangkok and Kota Kinabalu; Philippine Airlines runs direct flights from Manila, while Royal Brunei operates a service between Bandar Seri Begawan and Kota Kinabalu.

Although cruise ships call in at Kota Kinabalu on occasion, there is no regular shipping service to Sabah. A daily ferry plies between KK and Labuan, with the possibility of onward connections to Brunei or Limbang, Sarawak.

Visas

Valid passports are required for entry into Sabah. Like neighbouring Sarawak, Sabah has its own immigration control so even if you are coming from Peninsular Malaysia, you will be required to go through immigration and customs on arrival in Kota Kinabalu. Your passport must be valid for at least 6 months from the time of your visit to Sabah.

Visas given on arrival are normally for

Rural scenery west of Mt. Kinabalu

Playing a sompoton

30 days, and can be extended for another 60 days at the Immigration Department in Kota Kinabalu.

Citizens of Commonwealth countries, Ireland, Switzerland, the Netherlands and Lichtenstein do not need a visa to enter Sabah. The following countries do not need a visa for a visit not exceeding 3 months: Austria, Belgium, Denmark, Finland, France, Germany, Iceland, Italy, Japan, Luxembourg, Norway, South Korea, Sweden, Tunisia and USA.

Citizens from Israel and South Africa are not permitted to visit, while those from communist countries are granted visas from 7-14 days. Kampuchean and Vietnamese citizens are able to visit only on an official basis.

Customs

There is no duty-free allowance for visitors arriving from Peninsular Malaysia, Sarawak or Singapore. Those arriving from other destinations may bring in 250g of tobacco or cigars, or 200 cigarettes, plus a one-quart bottle of liquor.

Pornography, weapons and walkie-talkies are prohibited, while possession of narcotics and other illegal drugs carries the death sentence. Firearms are subject to licensing.

Vaccinations

Sabah enjoys a high standard of health and vaccinations are not necessary. Those staying in remote villages are advised to take malaria prophylactics, commencing the course in advance of arrival in Sabah. Visitors are required to produce a certificate of vaccination against yellow fever if they are travelling from an infected area.

Money Matters

The Malaysian currency is the Malaysian dollar or ringgit, which is divided into 100 cents (*sen*). You are permitted to bring in or take out unlimited amounts of Malaysian currency. Exchange rates fluctuate, but in late-1991, the rate of exchange was: US$1 = M$2.67; A$1 = M$2.02; £1 = M$4.98; S$1 = M$1.62.

Money changers offer the best rate of exchange for cash and travellers' cheques, and there is normally less waiting time than in banks. The latter give a better rate than hotels. Visitors are advised to change foreign currency in Kota Kinabalu before leaving for other areas of Sabah, where the exchange rate may be less favourable and facilities limited.

Credit cards are accepted at major hotels in Kota Kinabalu and other towns such as Sandakan, Tawau and Lahad Datu, as well as at a few restaurants in these locations. Cash, however, is a much safer proposition in most circumstances (and is essential for bookings at Sabah Parks.)

Clothing

Comfortable, cotton clothing is ideal for Sabah's tropical climate. Although dress is less conservative than in Peninsular Malaysia, women will feel more comfortable if they do not wear extremely short skirts or shorts, or tight, revealing clothing. For most situations, shorts or a skirt with tee-shirts or cotton shirts are ideal. A sun hat (which can be bought locally) and dark glasses are strongly recommended. If you are planning on climbing Mount Kinabalu, be sure to bring warm clothing, including an anorak, hat and gloves, as the temperature on the summit can drop below zero. A light raincoat or poncho may also be useful.

Trekking & Wildlife Observation

Many experienced local "jungle bashers" trek in shorts and tee-shirts; unless you are venturing through uncharted regions, it is not really necessary to wear trousers and long-sleeved shirts, which make you a lot hotter in the humid forest. Good trainers are preferable to heavy leather boots, as there is often a problem in keeping these dry. Leech socks (obtainable on the 1st floor of Sandakan Market and at Danum Valley Conservation Area) are recommended. The green-label Baygon insect repellent spray is the only one available in Sabah that is effective against leeches; spray around the ankles and feet, waist, neck and armpits. A light hat is also recommended. Be sure to bring a good pair of light field glasses, as well as a torch.

Electricity

The current in Sabah is 220 volts, 50 cycles. Electricity is available in all major towns and at most Sabah Parks' accommodation. A torch is recommended for travel to remote areas, and for use in the event of power failures.

Airport Tax

An airport tax of M$3 is payable for flights within Sabah, and to all other Malaysian destinations. The tax for flights to Brunei and Singapore is M$5, while to all other destinations, it is M$15.

Photography

The hot, humid climate of Sabah makes it advisable to carry your camera in a closed bag with sachets of silica gel to absorb the moisture. Print film is widely available in Kota Kinabalu and other towns. Standard transparency film such as

Kodachrome and Fujichrome is available in Kota Kinabalu, but if you want to use high-speed transparency film, it is advisable to bring it with you. Film processing for all but Kodachrome is available in major towns; you can even have 1 hour processing of prints done at the souvenir shop at Kinabalu Park.

Because of strong light in Sabah, you will obtain best results if you shoot before 10 am and after 4 pm, when colour density is better and side lighting gives you a more interesting picture. Most Sabahans are happy to have their photograph taken, but it is polite to ask first.